T0369753

Leading Generously

Leading Generously

Tools for Transformation

KATHLEEN FITZPATRICK

JOHNS HOPKINS UNIVERSITY PRESS

Baltimore

All rights reserved. Published 2024
Printed in the United States of America on acid-free paper
9 8 7 6 5 4 3 2 1

Johns Hopkins University Press
2715 North Charles Street
Baltimore, Maryland 21218
www.press.jhu.edu

Library of Congress Cataloging-in-Publication Data is available.
A catalog record for this book is available from the British Library.
ISBN 978-1-4214-4991-3 (hardcover)
ISBN 978-1-4214-4992-0 (ebook)

*Special discounts are available for bulk purchases of this book. For more
information, please contact Special Sales at specialsales@jh.edu.*

Neither tales of progress nor of ruin tell us how to think about collaborative survival.

—ANNA LOWENHAUPT TSING,
The Mushroom at the End of the World

There are a million paths into the future, and many of them can be transformative for the whole.

—ADRIENNE MAREE BROWN,
Emergent Strategy

It requires courage to let go of old certainties and experiment with a new worldview.

—FREDERIC LALOUX,
Reinventing Organizations

Whether on a small scale or in a large institution, our orienting political goal is to *build things*, whether institutions, norms, or other tools.

—OLÚFẸ́MI O. TÁÍWÒ,
Elite Capture

Contents

Leading Generously

Introduction

Between 2018 and 2020—before COVID-19 shut everything down—I had the opportunity to visit a number of college and university campuses where faculty, staff, students, and administrators had been thinking about how to create and support a greater sense of connection between their campus community and the publics that their mission statement and other founding documents indicated they served. The folks who invited me—ranging from the officers of campus chapters of the American Association of University Professors to university presidents and their advisors—seemed to feel a connection with the arguments I made about the future of the university in my book *Generous Thinking*, perhaps recognizing that their institution required not just a better strategic plan but deeper forms of cultural transformation in order to re-establish the public's faith in higher education. The transformation they sought, and for which I argued, demands a serious rethinking of how we work, why we work the ways we do, how we assess and reward that work, and how we recognize as work things that tend to get dismissed as service but that play a crucial role in building and sustaining collaborative communities. But, for whatever good *Generous Thinking* did (and I like to think it did a fair bit), there were nevertheless a few key gaps that remained in my thinking about how we should go about making that change.

For one thing, the turn that I had made between *Planned Obsolescence* and *Generous Thinking*—from an argument about the ways that scholars might better communicate with one another to an argument about the ways that scholars might better communicate with the publics that we serve—runs the risk of turning too much of our attention away from conditions on campus. Building

1

bridges between the academy and the communities around us is an important goal, but it can't be an *exclusive* goal. In fact, as Matt Brim notes in *Poor Queer Studies*, "we could ask whether breaking down the borders of the academy/community divide has substituted for and deferred intra-academic interrogations of class structure among the queer professoriate."[1] And not just within the queer professoriate, by any stretch. There are, after all, many campuses that have turned with gusto toward community engagement as a means of embracing their public mission. I'm delighted by those programs. Yet that work alone cannot transform a campus culture into one that is genuinely inclusive and equitable.

We must take a hard look at our internal engagements as well, and particularly at the hierarchies that divide us: between rich institutions and poor institutions, as Brim explores, but also between research faculty and teaching faculty, between faculty and staff. Between the white-identified folks who remain a majority of tenure-stream faculty and administrators and the Black and brown students we recruit—and the Black and brown colleagues we hire to support them and then fail to support in return. Between the secure and the precarious, in every respect. Dismantling those hierarchies and creating real equity demands something more than just generosity.

Related to that gap, moreover, is the fact that *Generous Thinking* focused pretty tightly on the *why* and the *what* of the changes I argued were needed in our campus cultures, and it spent far less time on the *how*. An example: it was clear to me then, and is even clearer now, that creating better, more sustainable institutions requires us to move away from quantified metrics for meritorious production—in fact to step off the Fordist production line that forever asks us to do *more*—and instead to think in a humane fashion about ways that we can do *better* and about exactly what it is we mean when we talk about "better," which often cannot be captured by the available metrics. These less calculable forms of better, of quality rather than quantity, frequently require slowing down, talking with our colleagues and our communities, and carefully considering what others have to say. Better requires engagement, connection, sharing, time, in ways that producing more nearly always encourages us to rush past. Turning from more to better can help us access the pleasures—and even the joys—of our work that life on the production line has forced us to push aside. But the ability to slow down is a privilege, and the kinds of career advancement providing that privilege are all bound up in *more*, making it increasingly unclear how we might open up the ability for *everyone* to slow down. Speed and busyness and exhaustion are the water in which we swim, so much a part of our environment that it becomes impossible to imagine changing them.

The question of how to begin the project of transforming campus culture and where to direct that effort had already persuaded me that I had a lot of follow-up work to do, that I needed to write something that would dig a bit deeper into the process of and the conditions for building something new. And then, after a talk I gave at Virginia Tech in October 2019, an attendee asked me what turned out to be a prescient question that's been stuck in the back of my head ever since: generosity is all well and good, she said, an idea that is relatively easy to embrace when we're flush, but how do we practice generosity in hard times? Can we afford to be generous when we're facing significant budget cuts, for instance, or is it inevitable that we fall back into analytics-driven competition with every unit—even with every worker—trying to protect its own resources and its own privileges?

I don't remember exactly how I answered then. I suspect it was some combination of "you're completely right; that's the real question" and "the difficulties involved in being generous in hard times are precisely why we need to practice generosity in a determined way in good times." And I may have said something about the importance of transparency in priority-setting and decision-making and of involving the collective in that process.

What I do know—as I stood there saying whatever I said—is that I was thinking, "wow, this is hard; I don't know." I don't know how we find the wherewithal to remain generous when times are bad, except by having practiced generosity enough to have developed some individual and institutional muscle memory for it and by recommitting ourselves to our basic values again and again. I especially don't know how we remain generous at a moment when our institutions approach us—we who work for them, as well as we who rely on them—and invoke the notion of a shared sacrifice that is required to keep the institution running. As Janine Utell reminds me, moments of crisis that are poorly handled can cause all of us—faculty, staff, and students alike—to lose faith in our institutions, as their commitments not only to the public good but to *our basic survival* come to seem shallow at best.[2] And those moments accumulate, with the resentment surfacing visibly in, for instance, the results of the 2022 Great Colleges to Work For survey, in which positive responses to the statement "There's a sense that we're all on the same team at this institution" declined by 7 percent from the 2021 survey, and negative responses increased by 6 percent, for a combined change of 13 percentage points in a single demoralizing year.[3]

I want our colleges and universities to survive, and I want to maintain the communities they enable, but I have seen firsthand that the shared sacrifice they call for in moments of crisis is never truly distributed equitably, nor is it equitably repaid once the crisis is past. I also know that however much I may want to keep my institution running, the institution is not thinking the same about me. Our institutions cannot love us back, and no matter how much we sacrifice for them, they cannot sacrifice for us. As with so many of my thoughts, this understanding was clarified for me by Tressie McMillan Cottom, who posted a Twitter thread describing the advice she gives to Black scholars who ask her how to survive in the academy. One tweet in particular stuck with me: "That is a pretty impolitic stance but I stand by it. I don't think these institutions can support us or love us. And I honor the many many people who work to make them more humane. But you, alone, cannot do that. And you cannot do it, ever, by killing yourself."[4]

It's not incidental that this advice comes from a Black woman speaking to other Black scholars, who in many cases were hired with the goal of creating greater equity within an institution but then are left to fend for themselves at the institution, which remains predominantly white. But the same is true for faculty members without tenure; it's true for the employees described in the US context as "support staff";[5] it's true for scholars working in contingent positions. It's true for everyone whose positions in the hierarchies of prestige and comfort leave them vulnerable, especially at moments when "we're all in it together" is invoked not in a context of resource-sharing but one of sacrifice.

Sacrifice tends to roll downhill, and to accelerate in the process. This is how we wind up with furloughs and layoffs among contract faculty and staff at the same time we find ourselves with a new associate vice-president for shared sacrifice.

If we hope to rebuild our culture's faith in our institutions of higher education, we have to begin by rebuilding *our* faith in them. We have to make them into the kind of team that we all *want* to be on—and then we have to ensure that *everyone* can play. We have to equip everyone not just with the knowledge and the skills necessary to make our colleges and universities work but also with the motivation to ensure that those institutions become great places to work. And all of this must begin with a deep, critical consideration of what our campuses have become. We have to ask what—and who—those campuses are for. We have to ask critical questions about what purposes they are intended to serve and how they are held accountable to those purposes. And we have to ask about how they are led—not necessarily about the *people* who lead them (though in some cases, that too) but rather about the *structures* through which they lead, the ways that decisions are made and priorities are set and the ways that communication within the institution is managed.

Structures are the key here. The only way to prevent anything from rolling downhill—even something as metaphoric as sacrifice—is to build structures that channel it differently. This is the deepest goal of *Leading Generously*: thinking with you about how we can build those new structures.

It's quite likely that the "you" I'm opening a conversation with is not someone with an upper leadership position in academia but is instead someone who, like me, cares enough about their institution to want to make it less awful for everyone. In this sense, *Leading Generously* is not for chancellors and presidents and vice-presidents, though I hope they find wisdom in it. It's for academic labor, for those on the front lines of executing the institutional mission. It's for middle management, the directors and chairs and deans who keep things going while taking flak from above and below. It's designed to give all of us who may feel powerless in the face of the institution's immovability some tools that might help us change it anyway.

This book is also not a conventional leadership guide, designed to teach you the skills you need to master in order to join the upper administrative ranks. Frankly, I'm far less interested in fostering new individual leaders who can rise through the ranks than I am in building cohorts and collectives, groups of grassroots leaders who can work together to transform the structures that support and constrain those ranks.

Leading Generously is focused on ways of thinking and being that might serve as general-purpose tools, rather than on a specific set of rules or tips or things to do. As a result, its advice, such as it is, needs to be practiced, day in and day out, in good times and in bad. That advice draws on the wisdom of those who have been organizing in the face of insurmountable odds for many years, people who have been surrounded by a white supremacist, patriarchal, capitalist culture that has objectified and oppressed them, and who have nevertheless persisted. In drawing on their wisdom I try to remain aware of the debt that I owe—that our institutions owe—and of what it would mean for our institutions to take the idea of repaying that debt seriously.

With all of that in mind, here's the core question shaping this book: If rebuilding faith in our institutions of higher education requires us to create a new understanding of and approach to leadership, then what new structures of leadership might help us remake our colleges and universities so that they can live up to their duty of care for all members of their communities, in good times and in bad?

There's a catch to that question, of course: the university is not going to remake itself. It has to be remade. And the "us" that I'm suggesting must do the remaking points to those members of the university community who are, to varying extents, empowered and motivated to take that work on. By the same token, it's unquestionably true that the empowerment and motivation of that "us" vary enormously, structurally, from position to position, from institution to institution.

Just four days after my 2019 talk at Virginia Tech, I spoke at a large public institution in the Midwest that had, hands-down, the most demoralized faculty I've ever encountered. The reasons for that state of despondency were painfully clear: they had an activist politician-turned-president who was bent on transforming the institution into a fully corporate enterprise and on undermining everything that tied the institution to the liberal arts, to critical thinking, to public service, to community. As a result, core academic departments had faced decade-long hiring freezes and were housed in buildings that were—and I suspect remain—literally toxic. The faculty members I talked to during my visit despaired of their inability to do anything with such a leader at the helm of their institution, much less with the board that hired him.

There's reason for despair in such circumstances, without question. But for whatever combination of reasons—privilege, thickheadedness, temperamental indisposition, sheer luck in the position in which I find myself—I'm not able to sit back and say, oh well then. *Leading Generously* is in large part about finding the things that we can do and the places where we might have some impact. Some of those places are internal: finding ways to engage in a deeper, more attentive manner with the work that our colleagues and students are doing and then drawing out what's best in that work to build upon rather than focusing on what it omits or fails at. Some of those places are external yet personal: finding ways to develop relationships with our colleagues, with our students, and with our communities that can open up our shared projects and turn them into a form of collective action. And some of these places are external and structural: finding ways to make it possible for others to engage in this kind of generous leadership as well.

In that sense, *Leading Generously* is intended to be a handbook for putting some of the ideas of *Generous Thinking* into action. It's also a means of putting the privilege that allows me to maintain what Rebecca Solnit might call "hope in the dark"[6] to work for others: while I recognize the immensity of the transformation that higher education needs today, I persist in believing that local changes can begin to make a difference and that we are capable of making those local changes.

That said, there are some important shifts in outlook that have taken root for me in the years since I wrote *Generous Thinking*, changes that cannot help but manifest themselves in this text. In the preface to that book I noted that I'd struggled as I was writing, especially through 2016 and 2017, to keep the book from becoming fundamentally angry.[7] While drafting *Leading Generously* between 2020 and 2022, and in particular while I revised in 2023, I became convinced that this struggle was utterly misplaced. Being raised a good, white, middle-class, Catholic girl in the deep South, I was taught that my anger was unacceptable; that it needed either to be transformed into something more productive or to be deeply internalized. I don't think I realized until recently the degree to which that message still haunts me, and yet given the state of the world today, and especially that of the United States, operating with the anger meter reading anything less than "full-on fury" feels impossible.

This is true of our political scene, which continues to degenerate by the day, even after a change in leadership in the executive branch; it's true of our cities and towns and streets, where the thin veneer of law and order has at last cracked wide open enough to force those of us with the privilege to have ignored it until now to reckon with the brutality that has always underwritten policing; and it's true of our institutions of higher education, too many of which throughout the multiple crises of the last few years have given every impression of placing institutional survival above the lives of those who work and learn on their campuses.

Given this widespread dereliction of duty by those who are meant to lead our nations and our cities and our institutions, nothing other than rage will do. I am trying to temper that rage into productive outcomes in this book, keeping in mind my hopes that we might work together to build a better place, but I feel obligated to note that such beating of emotional swords into ploughshares isn't easy. Our institutions have failed us. That much is clear. Equally clear is the extent to which our institutions have *been failed*, have been undermined internally and externally by a culture that does not believe in equity, that wants to ensure that sacrifice continues its downhill roll. As Timothy Snyder notes in *On Tyranny*, as flawed as they are, our institutions need us: "Institutions do not protect themselves. They fall one after the other unless each is defended from the beginning."[8]

To this I would add that there are moments when our institutions need protecting and defending from themselves. That is where I think we are in higher education today, and given that infuriating circumstance, I ask for your understanding. I hope to ask too for your vehement commitment, equal to your anger, to repairing the enormous damage that's been done—gradually over the decades, and then with increasing speed and visibility in recent years—by our institutions, which should always have been a model of generous thinking in action.

A Note on Method

The process of bringing this book into being was a bit idiosyncratic, neither drawing on the methods of close reading and analysis I was trained in as a scholar of literature nor adopting in any coherent sense the methods of another discipline. If anything, I drew on my long-standing blogging practice, which is to say I began by fulminating in a highly undisciplined way about something that bothered me and posted it online for feedback.

That feedback then led me both to a pile of prior literature that I needed to engage with and, more importantly, to a recognition that I needed to talk with actual leaders in higher education to find out more about their experiences and perspectives. As a result, I put out a call, both on my blog and through social media, for folks willing to talk with me. That call produced some good results, but the volunteers came mostly from the circles I was already embedded in. So I reached out directly to a variety of other leaders and asked them if they'd be willing to talk with me.

In the end, I conducted a total of 19 one-hour interviews over Zoom, and I began each one with the same request: "Tell me the story of your most important experience of leadership in the service of institutional transformation." I qualified this request by saying that the story could be one in which the interviewee was leading the process of transformation or one in which they learned from someone else who was leading it. Moreover, it could be a transformation that worked or one that didn't—whatever would be most instructive.

The leaders I talked with generously shared their stories and their ideas (and most importantly their time) with me. Many of them are named throughout this book; a few opted to remain anonymous. Across the board, their passion for what higher education ought to be inspired me.

I want to note, however, that this group of interviewees constitutes nothing like a scientifically determined sample. You'll notice that a disproportionately high number of folks work in and around institutional libraries, for instance. This skew in the set is due both to the fact that the library has been grappling with questions about leadership and institutional change in recent years and to the degree to which I've been in dialogue with librarians across my recent work.

You'll also notice that the majority of my respondents are white, and many of the institutions where they lead are predominantly white institutions. I sought interviews with a more diverse range of leaders in my solicitations, but few of the Black leaders and other leaders of color took me up on the offer. In many cases, they were too overtasked—as are minoritized leaders on all of our campuses—to be able to spare the time, especially for a request from someone they may know only secondhand. I take full responsibility for this shortcoming and recognize the work I still have to do in order to build the trusting network that real institutional transformation requires.

Once I competed a draft of the manuscript, I posted it to Humanities Commons, an online network for scholars and a platform for works-in-progress open to community review. Ten readers graciously provided their feedback, helping me to see the ways I was oversimplifying enormously complex problems, as well as the ways that my quite privileged and US-centered experiences had shaped my argument, to the detriment of true coalition-building. A long period of reading and reflection followed, which prepared me to tackle the revisions that were needed. I'm deeply grateful to those readers for their kindness and their patience, as well as to the unnamed reader whose review of the resulting revision was solicited by my publisher and whose generous questions (and excellent sense of humor) helped me sharpen several key ideas herein. The inevitable flaws remaining in what you now read are wholly my own.

PART I

The Problem

CHAPTER 1

Crisis

At this hour of the world, beginning a book about the state of higher education with an invocation of crisis is hardly unusual. In fact, it veers into the territory of cliché, so expected as to say practically nothing. And yet, given recent events at my own institution—as well, I suspect, at all of our institutions—to speak of the state of things without taking some time to dwell in the crisis seems all but impossible.

Many kinds of crises we talk about in academic life have been with us for quite some time, particularly those we experience in the shrinking corner of campus left to the liberal arts. The enduring nature of these conditions and responses to them has been described by Paul Reitter and Chad Wellmon in *Permanent Crisis*, which traces the long history of the rhetoric of crisis in the humanities back to the establishment of the German university system. That system gave shape to much of the structure of research universities in the contemporary United States, and many of its fights have likewise come to be ours. Reitter and Wellmon, in digging into that lineage, argue that the existence of the humanities in the modern era depends on our sense of crisis:

> For nearly a century and a half, claims about a "crisis of the humanities" have constituted a genre with remarkably consistent features: anxiety about modern agents of decay, the loss

of authority and legitimacy, and invocations of "the human" in the face of forces that dehumanize and alienate humans from themselves, one another, and the world. These claims typically lead to the same, rather paradoxical conclusion: modernity destroys the humanities, but only the humanities can redeem modernity, a circular story of salvation in which overcoming the crisis of modernity is the mission of the humanities. Without a sense of crisis, the humanities would have neither purpose nor direction.[1]

Whether this same sense of crisis and its causes can be extrapolated to the entirety of the academy is of course an open question, and yet it's easy to see the ways that contemporary decay, the loss of intellectual authority, and a general process of dehumanization have been the enemy of higher education writ large. Even at that scale it may be true that our sense of crisis, our sense of swimming against the cultural tides, has long given higher education its purpose.

There are, however, some features of the situation in higher education today—the threats that our institutions, our departments, our fields, and our researchers and instructors face—that are not simply rhetorical, and it's worth paying close attention to the specifics of these crises.

The labor crisis. Over the last couple of decades, we've watched as more and more good positions in the professoriate—with job security, an adequate salary, full benefits, and above all academic freedom—have been consigned to the gig economy. This ongoing "adjunctification" is happening across all fields on our campuses and is especially acute at the introductory levels, those areas of the curriculum meant to prepare students for anything that they go on to study. In fact, many of the community colleges and other two-year institutions that, in fall 2021, served over 30 percent of the undergraduate students in the United States do not provide their faculty members with significant job security at all;[2] those faculty often teach four or five courses per semester on year-to-year contracts. The effects of this labor crisis are manifold.

As fewer and fewer teaching faculty have the benefits of tenure,[3] and thus lack the voice in campus governance required to have a real impact on an institution's direction, undergraduate instruction is increasingly devalued in favor of grant- and publication-producing research. The more contingent the faculty's relationship to the institution becomes, the less commitment the faculty feel to the institution and the greater their identification grows with their subject-area colleagues elsewhere, increasing their abstraction from campus life. Service responsibilities are divided among fewer and fewer faculty, leaving them overburdened and at real risk of burnout. Worst of all, the hierarchical divides on campus—between tenured and untenured, between permanent and contingent, between faculty and staff—become deeper and wider.

This of course works hand in hand with **the economic crisis** that our institutions are mired in. As public funding provides a smaller and smaller portion of university budgets in the United States, the costs of higher education have shifted radically from the state and federal governments to individual students and their families. Other national university systems have recently been adopting, and increasing, student fees as well. As the costs of obtaining an education escalate, the pressure on students to think of a degree program as a market exchange grows. If they're going to sink tens, or even hundreds, of thousands of dollars into the purchase of a degree, it's not the least bit surprising that students would also face increasing pressure (whether internally, from their families or communities, or from commentators on television and the internet) to select a degree program that seems to promise an obvious career outcome. Thus majors that are named after jobs or industries grow, and those that aren't shrink, and anything that seems the least bit impractical or, heaven forbid, *critical* becomes a luxury that our institutions, like our students, cannot afford.

Third, there is **the political crisis**, which has been brewing for decades but has taken a particularly acute turn in the last few years. The attacks on critical race theory, the moves to ban books from libraries, the attempts to eradicate tenure, the direct interference in the curriculum, the closing of programs and departments and schools—all provide evidence of a growing backlash against the critical functions that higher education serves in the world.

And then there are myriad other crises, from the local to the global, that have surrounded us all in recent years.

At my own institution, Michigan State University, crisis has certainly come to seem a permanent state of being. I joined the faculty at MSU in August 2017, just before the news broke about the repeated and sustained sexual abuse and assault committed by Larry Nassar against hundreds of young women both at MSU and through USA Gymnastics. Our then president, Lou Anna Simon, came under intense critique and stepped down, if belatedly and reluctantly; the MSU board of trustees granted her a distinguished professorship and a yearlong research leave, at full presidential salary, after which she was expected to return to the faculty. However, in late 2018 she was charged with lying to investigators about her knowledge of the abuse—charges that were ultimately dismissed—and was placed on leave without pay.

That leave was imposed by our interim president, John Engler, a former Republican governor of Michigan, who was selected for the position by the board of trustees in January 2018 with no input from or communication with the faculty. Engler, who was described by the *Detroit Metro Times* as having "fought hard" during his governorship against claims made by victims of prison sexual abuse,[4] unsurprisingly came under protest for his callous treatment of Nassar's survivors and their families. He gave notice in January 2019 that he would step down from the presidency in a few weeks' time, but the board of trustees instead accepted his resignation effective immediately.

So we found ourselves with an acting interim president while the board searched for someone to lead the institution out of this morass. Samuel Stanley, then president of Stony Brook University, was named president in May 2019, and he set about the difficult task of trying to help the campus community heal and make the university a safe and welcoming environment for all. In September 2019, our then provost, June Youatt, stepped down after a Department of Education Office of Civil Rights report on the handling of the now multiple abuse cases at MSU—not only the sexual assaults perpetrated by Larry Nassar but also sexual harassment committed by his dean, William Strampel—revealed that she had failed to address complaints leveled at Strampel.

The search for a new provost was under way in March 2020, when the university made the abrupt transition to remote instruction as a result of the COVID-19 pandemic. I link those two events because I was on the search committee, conducting interviews in Detroit, when the announcement went out, at 10:00 a.m. on March 11, that MSU would move to remote instruction at noon that day. That is not an exaggeration: we were given two hours' notice. The 20-plus of us sitting in that hotel conference room included deans, chairs, directors, and other faculty and administrators with significant responsibility for ensuring the success of the academic mission. We managed what we could from a distance—a taste of what was ahead—then finished the interviews and headed back to East Lansing for what we hoped would be two weeks of working from home.

Needless to say, it did not turn out that way. While MSU was lucky to have a president who happened to be an infectious disease specialist—and so our early policies about remote instruction, working from home, and masking on campus were medically informed—we nevertheless faced a series of budgetary panics over the next two years, brought on by anxieties about whether students would continue to enroll. Like many other institutions, we experienced significant salary and benefits cuts, furloughs, and other austerity measures. Yet those panics turned out to be unnecessary; our enrollment remained strong, and between tuition income, federal support, and budget savings, the university wound up with a significant surplus. Some of that savings was eventually returned to employees but nowhere nearly as much as we'd been asked to give up.

I wish I could say that having weathered 2021 and 2022 marked the end of the crisis. But on a Sunday in September 2022, the faculty and staff found out from a story leaked to the *Detroit Free Press* that the board of trustees had given President Stanley until that Tuesday to step down before being fired.[5] This salvo not only caused grave concern among higher education leaders around the country about the board's interference in campus operations,[6] but it also set off waves of anxiety and anger on campus as everyone tried to figure out what on earth was happening.

For almost a month, a bizarre battle was waged through various statements and stories, each of which managed to make the situation less clear. Was the president under fire because he'd supported the provost, Teresa Woodruff, in her decision to relieve the dean of the business school of his duties after he'd failed to report incidents of sexual harassment? Or was it that President Stanley had failed to properly certify MSU's annual Title IX report? Did it have to do with the ongoing failures of the Office of Institutional Equity to handle abuse cases in a timely fashion? Or was it an internecine battle on the board being acted out through the media? The profound lack of transparency left everyone on and around campus guessing and finally resulted, in October 2022, in President Stanley submitting his letter of resignation and making a public statement in which he said he had lost confidence in the board and could no longer in good conscience report to them.[7]

Our provost, Teresa Woodruff, was named interim president in early November. She, like her predecessor, promised to work to heal the wounds that so many on campus had experienced. On February 13, 2023, however, new wounds became horrifyingly literal, when a masked gunman invaded an evening class and murdered three students, leaving five others in critical or serious condition. The entire campus was in lockdown for several hours that night, as law enforcement officers from MSU, East Lansing, several surrounding cities, and the State of Michigan searched the more than 500 buildings and 5,200 acres of our campus for the shooter, who shot himself upon being tracked to neighboring Lansing. The administration placed the university on emergency operations for two days and canceled classes for four to provide room for the investigation and allow time for students, staff, and faculty to grieve.

Even so, the return to campus was difficult. Debates roiled about whether campus buildings should be secured,[8] about whether students were ready to return to the classroom,[9] about whether there were sufficient counseling resources available for students and employees, and about whether any level of resourcing could ever be enough. There were vigils and marches and memorials and protests. Students testified before members of the state legislature, seeking gun reform legislation.[10] And naturally the administration's response was scrutinized—and many found it wanting.

The administration tried. They really did. The individuals in that mass of bureaucracy were just as hurt and sad and angry as any of us. But by the time communication made it through the available systems, it came out *official*. In the days after the shooting, faculty asking about remote instruction were told that no permanent changes would be made to declared course modalities. Students were informed about the policies through which they could declare a credit/no-credit option for the semester. And it was all wrong. Just wrong.

Just as this book went into production, in fall 2023, the board announced our new president, Kevin Guskiewicz, who would be coming to us from his position as chancellor of the University of North Carolina–Chapel Hill. President Guskiewicz is well versed in the challenges involved in running a public institution in an atmosphere of economic and political crisis, and my campus colleagues and I eagerly await his March 2024 arrival in East Lansing.[11]

———

This is *one* campus, over a *six-year* period. The crises MSU faced are particular in some ways—worse and more plentiful perhaps than those elsewhere—but they're not so different from things that have been happening on every campus in every state across the nation and on many campuses around the world.

I continue to believe that those of us who work in higher education can do better than this. I believe that we have at hand the means of responding to the external crises faced by our fields and our institutions, and of improving our responses to the internal crises we experience. I believe that we can demonstrate through the ways we go about our work a better path for the future of our institutions. I argued in *Generous Thinking*, for instance, for stronger connections between our institutions and the many publics we serve, as these connections might help facilitate a renewed sense of higher education as a public good. A range of forms of public scholarship, including community-engaged research and open publishing processes, might assist us as we build those connections.

But this isn't a simple proposition. Encouraging individual scholars to engage in more open, connected forms of scholarship requires deep institutional change to ensure that the work they do is valued and supported. Our institutions need not only to transform the ways that they weigh and reward public work, but they also need to adopt processes and platforms that can bring public work to life. As I'll argue in the chapters ahead, all of this requires a renewed commitment from us. Those of us who work for and care about our colleges and universities have to be willing to get active and organized on campus and begin developing the new structures that can enable our institutions to emerge from the current crises better than they were before.

Most important among those new structures is a new form of academic leadership. We need that new form of academic leadership not least because the crises in which we are mired demonstrate that the model under which we currently labor is irreparably broken.

I want to be clear in what I'm saying here: there are some very good people doing the best work they possibly can in many leadership roles on our campuses today. It's not the *people* that need replacing, or at least not *all* of the people, and, in fact, replacing them with new leaders with new visions has become an exercise of institutional deck-chair-rearranging while the ship continues to sink with the rest of us on board. The problem lies not with the people but with the systems within and through which they work. *That's* the model of academic leadership we need to contend with, a model with its boards and its presidents and its innumerable vice-presidents that comes to us directly from the hierarchical structures of corporate governance. Those structures are ill suited to the operation of nonprofit entities in general, as is argued by many of the folks involved in reimagining leadership for nonprofits today.[12] And those structures are doing grave damage to the purposes of higher education.

This is why our institutions' mission statements die a little bit every time someone says that the university should be run more like a business. That's because all of our institutions *already are* being run like businesses, and long have been. As Frederic Laloux argues, "The primacy of winning over purpose goes a long way in explaining why the 'mission statements' that organizations define often ring so hollow. . . . People have become cynical about mission statements because in practice they don't drive behavior or decisions. . . . So if the collective purpose isn't what drives decision-making, what does? It is the self-preservation of the organization."[13]

We've seen this impulse toward institutional self-preservation emerge through the crises of recent years, and it goes hand in hand with the assumption that the university should be run more like a business. Running a university like a business would mean that we'd keep a close eye on the bottom line, that we'd relentlessly pursue innovation, that we'd eliminate product lines not producing sufficient revenue, that we'd keep our front-line labor in check, and so on. All of which we've been subjected to for decades now, and all of which has contributed to the sorry state we're in.

Even worse, however, are the unspoken parts of "like a business," the individualist, competitive models for success fundamental to corporate structures: as Laloux has it, "winning over purpose." These reward structures are actively preventing our institutions from flourishing. This is true not just at the micro-level, where each individual student and employee and academic unit is required to compete for resources, but also at the macro-level, where our institutions are required to square off in the marketplace, in which competition is driven by rankings of winners and losers, rather than being encouraged to develop the cross-institutional collaborations that could lift the entire sector.

This is the bottom line: universities are not meant to be profit centers, and they shouldn't be run that way. They are, rather, shared infrastructures dedicated to a form of mutual aid, in which those who have—in this case, knowledge—support those who need, with the goal of producing a more just and equitable society.

Dean Spade defines mutual aid as "collective coordination to meet each other's needs, usually from an awareness that the systems we have in place are not going to meet them. Those systems, in fact, have often created the crisis, or are making things worse."[14] And as Peter Kropotkin argued at the turn of the twentieth century, mutual aid, mutual protection, and mutually beneficial cooperation have been as important to the development of both animal and human societies as the Darwinian mode of competition for survival. In fact, though history focuses on the role of conflict in societies—it makes for a more thrilling narrative than does cooperation—Kropotkin points to the significance of mutual aid to the ways we live and especially to the ways we learn: "the practice of mutual aid and its successive developments have created the very conditions of society life in which man was enabled to develop his arts, knowledge, and intelligence." He continues: "the periods when institutions based on the mutual-aid tendency took their greatest development were also the periods of the greatest progress in arts, industry, and science."[15]

Our campuses required mutual aid to be built, and their continued contributions to our society require mutual aid to sustain. As we move forward, we might even consider whether the ideal model for the university is not the corporation but the cooperative, in which every member has a stake in the successful outcome of the whole and is thus committed to full participation in its processes. First, though, we need to think about what we mean when we talk about leadership and how we might imagine a thoroughly different model of it.

CHAPTER 2

Leadership

"I really believe that the model of the single leader who carries everything themselves, who is heroic-seeming and so on, is super toxic, and outdated, and not working."[1]

This clear articulation of an idea that I'd spent months fumbling my way toward came from Dianne Harris, one of the people I was lucky enough to talk with at length about academic leadership. Harris is by any estimation a leader in the higher education universe. Her credentials include directing a large humanities center, serving as the president of a scholarly society, and working as a program officer for a major foundation, and she's now dean of the College of Arts and Sciences at the University of Washington. Across all of these roles, Harris has used her time and energy and influence to create alternatives to the ways that things are usually done, including initiatives for rethinking graduate education in the humanities and projects designed to build new forms of digital scholarly communication.

Harris is far from alone, either in her assessment of the toxicity of what we understand leadership to be within colleges and universities today or in her determination to find a better way. Yet all of us, Harris included, can look around at our institutions—not to mention the broader culture in which they are embedded— and recognize how ingrained the individualist model of leadership is and how hard it will be to change.

My goal is to lay the groundwork for transforming the model of leadership by which we're surrounded: to inspire the conversations and the gatherings and the plans and the actions necessary to reinvent academic leadership as something generative instead of toxic, something functional and flexible instead of obstructive. None of us can create that change in higher education on our own—but how we *can* create that change together is the focus of this book.

Leadership may seem a pretty odd subject for a professor of literature and digital media to write about. This book certainly wasn't on the list of projects I imagined lay in my future when my career began, but then neither did I imagine any of the strange turns that my career has taken. I've gone from writing conventional journal articles to exploring blogging as a scholarly form, from studying television and digital media to thinking about the ways networked communication might transform academic life, from being an unknown professor at a relatively isolated and small liberal arts college to being the first director of scholarly communication for the largest scholarly society in the humanities. I had no inkling that I'd find myself running a nonprofit scholarly network with nearly 50,000 users around the world or that I'd have the opportunity to build and lead a team in thinking about how that network could become sustainable without sacrificing its equity-oriented values. I could not have dreamed that I'd have the opportunity to serve as president of the board of directors of a small nonprofit organization as it reimagined and rebuilt its leadership structure. And I did not foresee the changes that would overtake institutions of higher education—or indeed the world—in recent years: deeper and deeper cuts in public funding for colleges and universities; astronomical expansion in student and family educational debt; a growing disbelief in education as any kind of social good beyond the individual, market-oriented credential it can provide.

Nor would I have dreamed that we would find ourselves, in summer 2020, watching as the leaders of colleges and universities struggled to decide whether to reopen their campuses in the midst of a deadly pandemic, a situation that was painfully repeated during another wave of COVID-19 infection the following year. I couldn't have imagined the kinds of political intrusion into campus governance across the United States that threatened not merely (*merely!*) to eliminate the protections of tenure but to eliminate programs and interfere in curricular decision-making. And I certainly couldn't have imagined watching my own institution's administration struggle to support students and faculty in the wake of a mass shooting—and they really did try—while nevertheless issuing directive after directive that wound up sounding unfeelingly bureaucratic to those most affected.

Martin Paul Eve asked me a crucial question in the open review of the draft of this book: "why do we believe that universities should be and do better than other institutions or places of work?"[2] Eve's question may have been rhetorical, but it points both to the importance of institutions of higher education in contemporary culture and to the ways that they repeatedly let that culture down. Universities should *do* better because they should *know* better. They should know better precisely because generating and sharing knowledge is the root of their purpose. And they should be better because their claims to focus on community should be backed by actual care for their actual communities.

Instead, we are experiencing a crisis in higher education that is bound up in a failed model of campus leadership and a misplaced understanding of what colleges and universities are for. If we are going to make it out of this crisis with institutions worth fighting for, all of us who work within those institutions need to reconsider what leadership looks like, how it should function, and most especially how we should contribute to it. If we are committed to the projects of knowledge creation and dissemination, of research and education in service to a better world, we have to begin by building better institutions. To do so, we need to cultivate and empower new kinds of leaders and give them new structures within which to work.

This is the goal of *Leading Generously*: to help those wanting to transform their institutional culture figure out how to begin. There are a lot of us on our campuses who want to see our institutions align their ways of working in the day-to-day with the visions and values that we espouse. We are folks willing to do the hands-on work of helping to build more generous institutions. While I'm expressly focused in the pages ahead on the context of colleges and universities in the United States, my hope is that the ideas in this book may also be useful to those who work in institutions of higher education outside the United States, as well as to those thinking about the need for change across many other kinds of institutions and organizations: educational and cultural, public and private, commercial and nonprofit. The only requirements for those institutions are that they understand themselves to be focused on creating a better world for everyone and that they are composed of people—whether their staff, their constituents, or their communities—who are willing to take the time, and make the effort, to reimagine and refashion their ways of working.

Those people are an institution's leaders, even if they're not the ones we conventionally think of that way. We often associate leadership with those select few executives at the top of an institutional hierarchy, those with the authority to steer the ship. Rather, as I'll discuss in the pages ahead, part of reconceiving leadership to escape the toxic model that so dominates our institutions today is understanding that everyone in an institution not only has the potential to lead but in fact has a key part in shaping the nature of leadership itself. The more we believe and act on the belief that anyone can begin the process of creating transformative change, the greater will be our opportunities for modeling better ways of being and for building institutions that are more supportive and sustainable.

This conviction is in part what led me to write this book. Traditionally, books on "how to lead" are written by authors who have held highly visible roles as leaders. They're present or former university presidents or chancellors, or corporate CEOs, or otherwise have direct experience with the responsibilities and challenges involved in directing a complex organization, and the advice that they share is valuable for those who wish to follow in their footsteps, who wish to attain and succeed in a similar high-level position. I haven't held such a leadership role on campus, at least not beyond that of department chair (for a small and relatively uncomplicated department) or center director (for a new research unit with a tiny budget), and as a result I don't seem like an obvious choice as a dispenser of academic leadership advice. I have had the privilege, however, of working with a number of administrators whose ideas about institutional transformation I've been able to witness taking root. Moreover, through my work leading Humanities Commons, as well as serving as president of the board of directors of the Educopia Institute, I've directly experienced a different side of leadership. I've found that when equity becomes a genuine commitment, and not just a talking point, developing new structures for organizational life becomes an imperative.

My goal, then, is to counter several pieces of conventional wisdom about leadership, perhaps most importantly that toxic model described by Dianne Harris: where the leader is a singularly powerful individual who sets the institution's course from atop the organizational chart. The heroic model of individual leadership is damaging not just to the institution, whose welfare is at the mercy of such an executive who must navigate an increasingly complex economic, cultural, and political landscape, but also to the well-being of that executive, who must convincingly appear omniscient and invulnerable and who will inevitably fail at pulling that off. We need a new framework for understanding leadership as collective and collaborative, rather than as individual, and therefore as a mode of connection that can be centered anywhere within the org chart where people have ideas about how to make things better. If we can come to appreciate and authorize the collective potential that exists within our institutions, we can begin to create institutions that are not only more generous but also more resilient.

There's a second bit of conventional wisdom that this book is working against, however, that seems to stand in opposition to the first. This idea posits the relative powerlessness of individuals in their encounters with the structures and systems of everyday life. Our sense of powerlessness derives both from some highly problematic sources—those who benefit from existing structures and systems and would prefer that everyone else just let them do their thing—and from some misunderstandings of recent critical theories regarding the ways that power operates in contemporary culture. Those theories—including arguments about race and racism; about sex, gender, and misogyny; about class and wealth—describe the issues they explore as *systemic* rather than *individual*. That is to say, they argue that real change requires social transformation. It requires building institutions, creating governments, enacting laws, and reshaping economies in ways that work toward equity rather than supporting privilege.

All of that demands something much larger, and much harder, than personal transformation. But we misunderstand the import of those theories if we assume they mean that individual action doesn't matter, that each of us is powerless. The individual matters, deeply—just perhaps not in the way we think.

When I argue that the complicated process of culture change can begin anywhere in the org chart, that any person (and not just the uniquely heroic leader) can be a change agent, I don't mean to suggest that the problems we face originate with individual behavior or that any given person's change of heart can change the world. But if our goals include building institutions that are structurally capable of supporting and facilitating the work of creating better communities and a better world, individuals have to find ways to claim power, because the institutions we have today aren't going to transform themselves.

It's a matter of where we locate agency, of who has the ability to make significant change in the world. If we understand power as residing in the structures and systems that govern our lives, or as the unique privilege of those with rank and status within those structures and systems, there is little agency left to the rest of us.

In what's ahead, my goal is both to counter the individualistic notion that leadership is a heroic, solo endeavor and to work against the idea that individuals are powerless. The problems we face today are enormous, and one person acting alone can't do much to change the world.

But groups of people can.

Groups of people working together can form coalitions and mobilize them to develop new organizational structures with collectivity at their center. Building those coalitions begins with the energy of individuals who decide to put their agency to work in solidarity with others.

That decision is a big one, and it often requires overcoming a great deal of resistance, both internal and external. Many ostensibly permanent faculty on college and university campuses don't particularly consider ourselves to be responsible for our institutions, in no small part because the institution is not our primary point of identification. We're often inclined to think of ourselves as free agents of a sort, at least theoretically able to pick up and move to another institution should a better opportunity arise, and thus consider ourselves and our work more accountable to colleagues within our own field than to colleagues down the hall (not to mention the next building over). The growing percentage of contingent faculty rarely have the chance to feel such a connection to their institutions, precisely because their institutions offer them no toeholds whatsoever, and therefore they have little to no opportunity for getting involved in institutional operations. Staff members often don't have the privilege of institutional mobility, and they rarely have the kinds of job security and other privileges that faculty receive. They frequently work in a coerced silence, either fearing for their livelihood if they speak out about inequities or other institutional problems or, worse yet, all too aware that their voices will be ignored. As a result, staff members frequently avoid sticking their neck out on issues that might get them into trouble.

The problem, of course, is that the crisis in institutional leadership that we face is enabled and exacerbated by our collective sense that fixing the institution isn't our job, that it should be left to the folks who are paid the big bucks to run things. But the retreat of faculty and staff into the work for which we are rewarded (or at least not punished), willingly handing off the running of our colleges and universities to an ever-thickening rank of upper administrators, has contributed mightily to getting us into this mess. The longer I stare at it, the more I believe that we, collectively—faculty, staff, and students as well—not only have the agency but also the responsibility to step forward, to take action, and to demonstrate that we belong to the institution as much as it belongs to us.

The people willing to step forward in this way are leaders, whatever their job title or position might suggest, and it's their leadership this book seeks to support.

So what do I mean when I talk about leadership? I don't associate leadership with rank or status or role; I don't connect it to authority; I don't think it has much to do with power or at least not the kind of power that we associate with individuals. In fact, I don't think leadership is something one possesses; it is rather something one practices: a habit of mind, a way of understanding the relationship among the self, others, and the world. It's a commitment to working with others toward transformation, and that commitment can be manifested at any level in an organization's hierarchy.

Of course, this is not how most of us experience leadership in our working lives. When we think of those who lead, many of us focus on the people at the top of the organization. Those folks up there—the presidents, the chancellors, the executive directors—are our institutions' leadership: they set the organization's course, they have the authority to speak publicly on its behalf, and they have the power necessary to make a difference in the ways the organization functions.

Perhaps. But I tend to think, more often than not, that referring to the individuals at the top of an org chart as "leadership" is a misleading euphemism. It's true that many of those people got to where they are because they are perceived to be leaders. But you'll notice that the cause and effect in the previous sentence is reversed from what you might expect: they got their jobs because they are, or appear to be, leaders; it's not the jobs that make them leaders.

In fact, most of what comes to us from above in our institutions and organizations is management rather than leadership. Numerous experts in business and management argue that leadership is profoundly misunderstood in contemporary culture.[3] For instance, John P. Kotter, the Konosuke Matsushita Professor of Leadership Emeritus at Harvard Business School, argued in the *Harvard Business Review* that management and leadership are distinct though complementary modes of organizational action. In his framework, management is focused on "coping with complexity," on organizing and directing the people and resources necessary to conduct an organization's work. Leadership, by contrast, is about "coping with change," the more ambiguous work of setting new directions and helping move people toward them.[4] The distinction is significant for Kotter, not least because of his conviction that most organizations today are "over-managed and underled."[5] Even more, Adrienne Kezar notes the extent to which many positional leaders in higher education fail to understand the nature of change, either treating it as a formulaic, top-down process or, worse, ignoring it as it happens around them.[6] At every level of our institutions, we have arguably been organized and disciplined into an inability to cope with—much less create—change.

Similarly, Peter Senge, author of *The Fifth Discipline* and senior lecturer at the MIT Sloan School of Management, observes that "the very word 'leader' has come to refer largely to positional authority, a synonym for top management."[7] The danger in this, for Senge, runs deep, not least because, as he argues, "the prevailing system of management is, at its core, dedicated to mediocrity. It forces people to work harder and harder to compensate for failing to tap the spirit and collective intelligence that characterizes working together at their best." His goal, in guiding institutions to become what he calls "learning organizations," is the development of "an alternative system of management based on love rather than fear, curiosity rather than an insistence on 'right' answers, and learning rather than controlling."[8] This alternative system of management, and its emphasis on learning—so completely at odds with what most of us experience as part of organizations—has a lot in common with the kinds of leadership that I argue institutions of higher education need today.

Kotter and Senge, while visionary, are not wholly outliers in theorizing management culture. Edgar Schein and Peter Schein, coauthors of *Humble Inquiry* and cofounders of the Organizational Culture and Leadership Institute, describe a similar conception in their preface: "Our culture emphasizes that leaders set direction and articulate values, all of which predisposes them to *tell* rather than *ask*. Yet it is such leaders who may need Humble Inquiry most because intricate interdependent tasks require building positive, open, and trusting relationships above, below, and around them, in order to facilitate safer and more effective task performance and innovation in the face of a perpetually changing context."[9]

As a culture, we have collectively placed an enormous emphasis on the singularity of leadership, on the leader as a strong individual who possesses something we call "vision." In fact, "vision" has turned into such a leadership cliché that it's become the determining focus of search committees for upper administrative positions, despite the fact that candidates usually know little about the institution they seek to lead. As Dianne Harris told me,

"If someone comes in [during the search process] and tells you what their vision is, I don't think you should hire them."[10] Similarly, Marjorie Hass, author of *A Leadership Guide for Women in Higher Education*, notes that she has known leaders "who announce a vision as soon as they land on campus. These are usually people who are more focused on the kind of leader they are than on the kind of institution they are leading."[11] No prospective new hire, no matter how visionary, can possibly know your institution and its complexities well enough from the outside to tell you where you ought to go.

Moreover, vision is, in this structure, always a top-down affair. As Ronald A. Heifetz and Donald L. Laurie argue, solutions to the deepest challenges faced by institutions today don't always issue from the chief executive's office, and yet everything about the hierarchy built around that office reinforces the mistaken expectation that it is the seat of wisdom: "the prevailing notion that leadership consists of having a vision and aligning people with that vision is bankrupt because it continues to treat adaptive situations as if they were technical: The authority figure is supposed to divine where the company is going, and people are supposed to follow."[12] This is, in Heifetz and Laurie's view, both a failure to understand the complex nature of the challenges that institutions face today and a failure to understand the primary work of leadership as connective and interpersonal rather than authoritarian and managerial.

At base, our understanding of leadership, as Rae André suggests in *Lead for the Planet*, stems from the individualistic and possessive biases of Western culture. The dominant strain in conversations about leadership, including in business schools, is determined, she says, by "competency theory—the study of individual traits and skills."[13] Within that theory, leadership is understood as a skill that an individual person either has or develops, and competency in leadership is something that the individual then puts to work on their own.

As with other individual competencies, leadership skills are not imagined to be equally distributed. There's a decided skew toward whiteness and maleness and abled-ness and wealth and an elite education—not just in our outward assumptions about those we expect might be leaders but often in our inward assessments of our own capacities for leadership. Too many of us look around at the chaos of our lives, and the relative lack of individual agency we experience in our jobs, and decide that we're in no place to consider ourselves anything like leaders, much less to enact leadership.

That's not just a personal problem; a contributing factor in many of the problems that higher education faces as a sector may well be the extent to which the vast majority of us feel closed out of leadership by our roles or by our identities or by our personalities or by the systems within which we work. What makes it a problem has less to do with some sense in which we're not living up to our individual potential than with the reality that the institutions within which all of us work are deprived of the collective ideas, energy, enthusiasm, and conviction that could guide them.

Threaded through the critiques of conventional leadership outlined above, a common issue might come to our notice: the individualism with which contemporary business culture understands what it is to be a leader. Several of these thinkers point toward a more collaborative ethos as the grounding for their view of leadership, and yet in the end the leader is still singular, still authoritative, still the person behind the desk where the buck stops. We know this to be true in higher education; too often what passes for collaboration in academic institutions is in fact coercion with a smiling face. It's this mode that leads Barry Bozeman and Michael Crow to argue, in *Public Values Leadership*, that "[t]he stuff of leadership is to a large degree the ability to envision rationalizations for action that will resonate with others and will motivate collective action."[14]

True collaboration in leadership is not about getting people to do what you want. It's about working with people to determine what's best for everyone involved and how you might build toward your collective goals together. This can be true even if you're a positional leader with the responsibility to move an organization forward. As adrienne maree brown advises in *Emergent Strategy*, "If you are in a leadership position, make sure you have a circle of people who can tell you the truth, and to whom you can speak the truth. Bring others into shared leadership with you, and/or collaborate with other formations so you don't get too enamored of your singular vision."[15] Even better, that collaboration might help break down your vision's singularity, making it genuinely shared.

Shared leadership may seem at first like an oxymoron in today's individualist, capitalist culture, but it might help point the way to more productive engagements with organizational life. After all, beneath the surface, all leadership is to some extent shared, and turning with intention to its collective aspects could provide relief from the constraints within which we operate today. Sayeed Choudhury, director of the Open Source Programs Office in Carnegie Mellon University Libraries, noted in an interview with me that while "the person leading, or even the people leading" in any given organization are important, we need to think about "the culture, the systems, the processes in place, the policies," all of which he collectively described as the "leadership infrastructure." Like the other kinds of infrastructure we more commonly imagine—roads, electrical grids, communication networks—the leadership infrastructure in a given organization is often easy to overlook and yet bears within it the possibilities for making things happen. It also presents the "bounds and constraints" that limit that work. "You can't push this organization beyond the boundaries of what its leadership infrastructure can handle," Choudhury pointed out. The most important work of collective leadership must be focused on expanding those bounds and constraints, on "getting away from that hero leader model" and instead ensuring that "leadership has permeated throughout."[16]

Leadership of this sort, which is focused not on individual authority but rather on creating a more inclusive, more resilient infrastructure, asks us to model and to create the conditions for better ways of working, not just by or for ourselves but in community with those around us. Beyond creating that resilient infrastructure, however, collective leadership calls on us to use the culture, the systems, the policies and processes at our disposal in order to bring out the best in others and help bring them into leadership too. Leadership of the sort I propose focuses on developing the relationships necessary for collective action. It's connective and compassionate and generative. And it can emerge anywhere in an institution, if cultivated.

I choose the metaphor of cultivation pointedly, with deep thanks to Beronda Montgomery, whose brilliant book *Learning from Plants* explores the ways that an understanding of botanical life can help us develop more productive, more supportive, more collectively attuned ways of working in human communities. As Montgomery argues, such an understanding encourages us to focus on remediating the environments in which we work together rather than attributing the difficulties some individuals experience in taking root and growing in those environments to internal deficits. This approach also calls on us to develop a new kind of leadership vision, one that can

> adapt to changing circumstances, and . . . enable leaders to see the potential collaborations and benefits in diverse communities. This approach contrasts with the traditional gatekeeping approach, in which leaders determine who gains access via conceptualizations and assumptions about who can function and thrive in a particular context. Instead, this distinct form of leadership is sense driven and environmentally adaptive; it attends to individuals while at the same time tending the ecosystems in which these individuals exist. I call this form of leadership groundskeeping, in recognition of what we know about the conditions that plants need to successfully thrive.[17]

Groundskeeping rather than gatekeeping. Cultivation rather than constraint. These organic metaphors allow us to think about leadership as something that is grown and not something that is possessed, entailing an awareness that our institutions and organizations are more akin to ecosystems than they are to the org charts we draw to represent them. Our leaders must work in concert with their ecosystems, rather than operating from the management perspective once known as "command and control."

Are our institutions as they are currently structured even capable of fostering such an organic mode of leadership? Some are, but significant work was very likely needed to make them so. For most of our institutions, the reality is far different, I'm afraid. It's not accidental that Dianne Harris referred to the most common model of leadership in higher education as "toxic"; not only does it fail to work the way we'd like it to, but it also tends to poison the ground around it and prevent anything new from taking root.

Part of the problem, as Harris noted, is the organizational structure predicated on the single-leader-at-the-top. Such leaders are given both too much responsibility and too much authority, a situation that's counterproductive for them and detrimental to their organizations. As Deborah Ancona, Thomas W. Malone, Wanda J. Orlikowski, and Peter M. Senge argue, our organizations ask and expect too much of the folks at the top of the org chart:

> Top executives, the thinking goes, should have the intellectual capacity to make sense of unfathomably complex issues, the imaginative powers to paint a vision of the future that generates everyone's enthusiasm, the operational know-how to translate strategy into concrete plans, and the interpersonal skills to foster commitment to undertakings that could cost people's jobs should they fail. Unfortunately, no single person can possibly live up to those standards.... [T]he sooner leaders stop trying to be all things to all people, the better off their organizations will be.[18]

Ancona and her colleagues present instead the notion of the *incomplete leader*: as executives recognize that they can't be everything to everyone, they might come to rely on others to help fill the gaps.

"Well, *duh*," I can hear every president and executive director the world over respond: "This is why I have a leadership team!" And yet the vast majority of those leadership teams—especially where they are colloquially referred to as the "C-suite"—function as reinforcement for the centrality of the chief executive; as the phrase has it, team members serve at the pleasure of the president.

The president's vision and authority remain dominant, and the executive team remains more hierarchical and competitive than collaborative.

Of course, the president's vision and authority only remain dominant *to an extent*: the president is hired by and responsible to a board, and as the board's sole employee, the president bears the full weight of that governing body's pleasure or displeasure on their shoulders. Relationships between boards and administrations are too often codependent or toxic as a result. Boards frequently do not know or abide by the boundaries of their role, taking the term "governing" much too literally. While it's true that boards of directors are written into nonprofit law as a required part of the governance structure of such organizations, the ways those boards function and the relationships they build with the organization's executive and operational staff are not mandated. In fact, what is generally mandated is not the board's power but its responsibility: board members have a fiduciary duty to ensure that the organization uses its resources wisely and serves the public interests for which it was founded. In the case of state colleges and universities, the board—of trustees, of visitors, of governors, or what have you—may have been given more explicit authority in the laws that created the institution, and those laws may be difficult to revise, especially in the current political environment. But even in such cases, a new understanding between the board and the institution can lead to a more collaborative relationship, one in which the board supports the organization in achieving its goals rather than interfering or dictating.

Such a collaborative relationship would support new modes of shared leadership that don't hang the full weight of leading on a single chief executive. It's worth asking, in fact, whether our institutions really need a president and whether the roles that the president serves might in fact work better if shared among the members of a true leadership team who are responsible to one another, are required to work collectively to make decisions, and are accountable to the rest of the institution for its success.

I noted near the end of the previous chapter that, given the resemblance between institutions of higher education and organizations founded for the purposes of mutual aid, the ideal governance structure for colleges and universities bears more in common with the cooperative than the corporation. In collective models like that of the co-op, leadership is of necessity coalition-based rather than hierarchical. It is built from relationships and built to sustain relationships. But experiments with shared leadership have been conducted within corporate structures as well. Ancona and colleagues describe such a model as employed in a large Dutch consulting firm: "A few years ago, it replaced the role of CEO with a team of four managing directors who share leadership responsibilities. . . . Clearly, for [this] senior team model to work, members must be skilled at engaging in dialogue together. . . . [B]ecause each director can veto a decision, each must thoroughly explain his reasoning to convince the others that his perspective has merit."[19] Shared leadership models such as this cultivate a team's interdependence, requiring each member to develop not just their relationship with the boss but their mutual relationships with one another as well, relationships that form the basis of the institution's success.

This is true at every level in an institution: our collective success at the department level, the college level, and the university level all depends upon our becoming and acting as a collective, upon our developing and relying on the relationships that can enable us to establish and achieve the shared goals we hold most dear. And that process—of determining what our shared goals should be and how we should move toward them—requires a kind of interrelation that is not merely personal but also, and of necessity, political.

––––––

I quoted from Tressie McMillan Cottom's *Lower Ed* in the epigraph to the last chapter of *Generous Thinking*, which focused on the need for rethinking the university to make it a more just institution. Here is that quotation again: "This is not a problem for technological innovation or a market product. This requires politics."[20] That idea—that we cannot simply innovate ourselves out of the problems we face in higher education today but instead must reckon with the underlying inequities and disparities that led us, and keep us, here[21]—resonated with me immediately, but it's taken me a long time to arrive at some of its deeper implications. This is in part due to my tendency to read the word "politics" superficially. It's true after all that we need to appeal to the voting public and the representatives they elect in order to effect real transformation in the legal and economic frameworks within which higher education is today constrained.

But the import of McMillan Cottom's use of the term "politics" should not be contained by thinking just about the realm of elected government. Nor do the more casual ways the word describes internecine machinations among groups in an organization—as in "office politics"—reveal what's really at stake. The politics that can transform the university requires a deeper understanding of the relationships that drive our institutions and so must encompass more than the structures and policies that govern them.

In *Justice and the Politics of Difference*, Iris Marion Young defines "politics" as "all aspects of institutional organization, public action, social practices and habits, and cultural meanings insofar as they are potentially subject to collective evaluation and decisionmaking."[22] The word "potentially" is doing a lot of work here; in most of our lives, those structures, actions, practices, and meanings are not subject to a kind of decision-making in which we're encouraged to play a real role. However, Young later notes that "the concept of justice coincides with the concept of the political," arguing that every effort must be made to enhance collective evaluation and decision-making if we are to create the possibility for just institutions.[23] And just institutions must be our goal.

In most colleges and universities, the potential for "collective evaluation and decisionmaking" is contained within the structures of shared governance on campus. Those bodies, including a range of working groups, committees, and senates, serve to gather faculty and (in some cases) staff opinions on many questions concerning the operation of the institution. On a few such questions—for instance, the curriculum—those bodies exercise a kind of ownership, and the decisions issuing from them have the mark of authority. On many campuses, however, and on many issues, faculty and staff governance is advisory at best: votes are taken, decisions are made and communicated, and that's it. The institution's administration has the freedom to take those resolutions up and act on them, or to ignore them at will. And as Martin Eve reminds me, the shared governance processes of many public institutions are constrained by legal restrictions that give the board an inviolable final say.[24] In such circumstances, shared governance can devolve into busywork, or worse; as Evviva Weinraub Lajoie told me, the processes of shared governance performed without an ethical commitment to sharing power can turn into "a toxic cudgel that doesn't benefit anybody."[25]

In many cases, the collective deliberation and decision-making bodies that form the core of shared governance have become less political, in Young's sense, than they are bureaucratic, functioning in order to function rather than bearing the potential for change. Bureaucratic organizations, in Young's understanding, are tasked with implementing and enforcing policies, but in most cases they do not have the power to set those policies, and they have little leeway in how they are applied. "Bureaucracies," Young notes, "are distinguished from other forms of social organization in operating according to impersonal rules that apply in the same way to all cases."[26] The importance of these rules and the processes and functions through which they are applied should of course not be dismissed; as Young goes on to note, bureaucracy as we experience it at the level of the state developed in order to replace individual sovereignty and its less rational whims with the rule of law. Similarly, the principles and processes of shared governance serve to mitigate the unjust imposition of a top administrator's opinions on faculty and staff functions. But an overreliance on and even subjugation to those principles and processes runs the risk of making the bureaucracies through which we operate seem politically neutral and eternal and unchangeable.

As Young points out, "the values of bureaucratic organization" indicate that decisions should be made "according to merit." This reliance on merit in bureaucracy is, she notes, among "the important positive developments in the history of social organization."[27] What is missing, however, is a deep engagement with and debate concerning the meaning and determination of *merit itself*. Our institutions have devised metrics and methods that allow us to believe that merit is a quantifiable thing we can assess outside the realm of the political. But merit as a category is always and inevitably ideological, in the sense that it provides a commonsense explanation that transforms highly contingent relations of domination into something natural or neutral. As Young argues:

> The rules and policies of any institution serve particular ends, embody particular values and meanings, and have identifiable consequences for the actions and situation of the persons within or related to these institutions. All of these things are open to challenge, and politics is the process of struggle and deliberation about such rules and policies, the ends they serve, and the values they embody. The ideology of merit seeks to depoliticize the establishment of criteria and standards for allocating positions and awarding benefits.[28]

That depoliticization sounds like a good thing—by making the awarding of benefits as objective a process as possible—until we remember that the individual people involved in defining and implementing a meritocracy are not and can never be objective. We are all inescapably subjective, bringing our own experiences and perspectives to everything we judge. What depoliticization means in the bureaucratic, and particularly in the meritocratic, is a closing-off of the opportunities for debating the criteria, the processes, and the objectives through which we might keep notions like merit from becoming tools of oppression. As it becomes depoliticized, bureaucracy errs in treating the rules as the *ends* that it seeks, rather than a *means* to those ends. Even more: the bureaucratic reliance on notions like merit fails to consider either the degree to which preexisting privilege clears a path toward (or is even mistaken for) meritoriousness or the self-perpetuation of merit when it is assessed by those previously deemed to have it. As Olúfẹ́mi Táíwò argues in *Elite Capture*, for an organization or a process or a structure to become genuinely anti-oppressive, it must engage in a constructive politics, working to build better social systems by paying attention not simply to the ways that the people already in the room engage with one another but also to dismantling the room and building a better one.[29]

Take, for example, peer review. I've written extensively elsewhere about the problems endemic to today's conventional peer review, and I won't rehash all of that argument here.[30] But one key point has to do with the role that anonymity plays in the process. As is frequently noted, the practice of anonymizing submissions that undergo peer review for publication, in journals and by university presses, was established to mitigate the influence of reviewer bias based on the gender, race, institution, or other characteristics of the author. Similarly, reviewer anonymity was designed to permit reviewers with lower career status to criticize the work of higher-status scholars without fear. These goals were and remain admirable—as they train attention on the quality of the work and allow that quality to be assessed without reserve—and their success has been appreciable. Author anonymity permitted the work of minoritized scholars to gain purchase in the highest levels of academic discourse, and reviewer anonymity allowed new perspectives to counter established orthodoxies.

What anonymity did not do, however, and cannot do, is *eliminate bias*, which will always find ways to creep back in around the edges. Critiques of subject matter or methodology or cited sources become proxies for status based on identity and serve as arguably neutral means of reinforcing hierarchies within fields. Again, my intent here is not to discount the importance of establishing and following the rules and procedures that have developed for vetting scholarly work. Rather, I want to note that those rules and procedures can never provide for the fullness of justice, precisely because the rules and procedures are treated as if they are sources of objectivity when they have inevitably been designed and are always implemented by individuals with inescapable subjectivities.

Moreover, trying to change the rules and procedures to make them *more* objective is laudable, but it cannot help but introduce new areas in which objectivity comes into question. Ultimately, as Young argues, the goal should be not to exclude subjectivity or "personal values" from decision-making but rather to make that subjectivity and those personal values fully part of the decision-making process, as these values are "inevitably and properly part of what decisionmaking is about."[31] So instead of trying to make peer review more bias-free—a worthy but ultimately fruitless effort of depoliticization—perhaps we might alternatively accept its deeply political nature, make it more transparent and participatory, and ask authors and reviewers alike to surface and contend with their values as a part of the process. Perhaps we might, as Rebecca Kennison suggests, turn from peer *review* to peer *engagement* as a means of bringing colleagues together to improve the work collectively.[32]

Similarly, we might rethink the ways that tenure and promotion processes and policies are implemented. These bureaucratic formations have been designed to protect candidates from the whims or animus of administrators as cases move through the approval hierarchy. And yet that bureaucracy has the potential to interfere with justice in its requirement that all cases be treated identically rather than respecting their particularities and differences. As Young notes of the gap between bureaucracy and truly democratic collective action, "Decisions and actions will be evaluated less according to whether they are right or just than according to their legal validity, that is, whether they are consistent with the rules and follow the appropriate procedures."[33] This concern for form is encoded in the process for appealing denials of promotion and tenure at many institutions, where the acceptable range of inquiry is restricted to whether the evaluation was properly conducted according to the predefined rules, rather than whether the final determination was just, and much less whether the process as constituted was capable of producing a just result.

Changing how peer review is conducted so as to surface rather than avoid reviewer bias would, one might reasonably argue, make peer review political. And, similarly, changing the grounds for appealing the decisions of review committees to include the justice of their outcomes—or even better, changing the criteria for promotion and tenure such that they surface and embrace their subjectivity rather than assuming an unearned impartiality— would likewise make those decisions political. And yet it's clear to just about everyone who has ever been through peer review or come up for tenure, especially from a nondominant position within the academy, that those processes and decisions *have always been political* and will always remain so. That's not in and of itself a bad thing. We should not want to remove politics from the ways that we engage with one another on campus; rather, we should consider creating an environment in which we can embrace a collective, coalitional politics, rendering all of us able to participate—and responsible for participating—wholly and with an open and honest intent in the processes through which our working lives are inevitably structured.

So what does this have to do with leadership? I raise the question of the political because all of the ideas and bits of advice that follow in this volume require politics.

Let's return for a moment to the distinction I drew between management and leadership. If management, as Kotter characterized it, is focused on "coping with complexity," on ensuring the optimal functioning of entangled structures and organizations, we might begin to intuit a relationship between management and bureaucracy. Establishing rules and processes, ensuring that they're followed, remediating them when they fail, all require careful management. In associating management with bureaucracy I do not at all mean to dismiss the importance of good management, as can anyone attest who has ever worked with a poor manager; as one leader I talked with reminded me, there's a real value in keeping the trains running on time.[34] But if management is about ensuring that things get done with maximum efficiency, it's also about eliminating or at least minimizing everything that can interfere with that efficiency, including—and perhaps especially—dissent. Management is in this sense necessarily depoliticizing; it requires foreclosing debate and smoothing the way for prescribed action. This is one reason why the good management needed for making the status quo function often has difficulty contending with change: when an organization tries to manage change, it too often ends up with a manufactured consent that squelches the political and moves decision-making outside the realm of debate. This is true not just of institutions but of a wide range of projects and organizations that seek consensus. As Evviva Weinraub Lajoie framed it, "I struggle with the open-source ethos of 'if you want to engage, just show up!' It's really not that easy"—not least because just showing up is hard when dissenting voices aren't welcomed.[35]

If leadership, as Kotter contrasts it with management, focuses on "coping with change," then good leadership must of necessity be political at heart. Leadership does not just require accepting but in fact embracing and facilitating the kinds of open debate, dissent, and even struggle necessary for making the best possible decisions about what an organization should do and how it should do it. Leadership requires making room for the broadest possible participation in decision-making, and it requires developing the relationships and coalitions necessary to ensure that the resulting decisions are understood and embraced. Leadership is about creating the conditions necessary for the many people within an organization to contribute to and feel ownership of the organization's future. And that work is utterly dependent on and congruent with politics.

This is not to say that all organizations can be effectively run by consensus. Most of them can't, and where well-meaning leaders try, the consensus is often produced by suppressing or ignoring dissent. Where consensus fails, the need for an embrace of the political nature of leadership becomes acute. Positional leaders are all too frequently called upon to make decisions that are bound to be unpopular with a significant portion of the people they affect. In these cases, it's all the more important that the decision-making process be transparent; that those affected have real cause to believe that their input has been heard; and that they are given insight into the process by which, and the reasons why, the final choice was made. That knowledge won't make everyone happy— a difficulty with which leaders must be ready to contend—but it creates the best possible chances for avoiding the breaches of trust that undermine relationships and make leadership impossible.

Change is hard, and coping with it requires more than just positional authority; it requires deep relationship building, a willingness to listen, a commitment to transparency, and an ability to inspire and maintain trust. All of these aspects of leadership might remind us of the reasons why the most effective politics is often conducted at the grassroots level, through real engagement with people and their needs and fears in the day to day.

The chapters that follow in part II explore a set of tools that might enable us to work together in developing a new model of leadership in higher education that centers collaboration and connection. They're not tools in the conventional sense of most leadership training; there are no mnemonics or matrices to facilitate your planning or structure your workflow. But they're tools nonetheless, ways of centering your work and yourself as you work in order to help you live out the ethical commitments you want to bring to your institution. In describing these tools, I draw on my own experiences as well as the wisdom of the higher education leaders I've had the privilege of speaking with over the last couple of years. Following the tools are a few brief stories in part III that show the tools in action. You can read these chapters on tools and stories in any order that appeals to you, though they build on one another as they go. Here, however, is a preview, a tl;dr of what's ahead:

- Remember that what leadership leads is not an organization but **people**.
- Leading people begins with doing some hard work on **yourself**.
- You can't change the world alone, but we can do it **together**.
- Building coalitions requires a willingness to reveal your **vulnerability**.
- Collectivity also demands the cultivation of deep, multi-directional **trust**.
- Shared governance requires a collective understanding of shared—and sometimes conflicting—**values**.
- Collective understanding must begin through a program of deep **listening**.

- Maintaining trust in shared governance requires designing processes with a commitment to **transparency**.
- Ensuring that an organization is flexible enough to work through future challenges requires **nimbleness**.
- Describing and assessing institutional goals requires not just data but **narrative**.
- An institution's service to the public good can only be as strong as its understanding of **sustainability**.
- Turning a campus into a community requires more than lip service; it requires real **solidarity**.

In elaborating on each of these ideas, I hope to create a picture of leading an institution toward transformative change that is less about managing a project or people and more about building shared solutions to shared challenges. Making such a possibility real depends on our collective commitment to thinking together about what our institutions could become if we were to center equity and to develop new structures for truly shared leadership within them.

Questions for Reflection and Discussion

The idea for this book surfaced in part in a discussion about the possibility of a how-to guide to implementing the principles behind *Generous Thinking* and was further clarified in a series of workshops and reading groups that I participated in after the book's release. I suspect that, given the work of coalition building that's at the heart of the new model of leadership I espouse here, you may want to read and discuss this book with a group—whether composed of the colleagues you're seeking to build a coalition with or a more dispersed set of coalition builders.

In either case, this chapter and each of the chapters in part II, "The Tools," concludes with a few questions that might jump-start your discussion.

- What do you consider your most formative experience of leadership? This could be an experience in which you were the leader or in which you worked under someone else's leadership. What were your goals, and how did this moment of leadership work toward them?

- What experiences do you have of problematic or even failed models of leadership? What kept them from working as they should?

- What lessons have you taken from these experiences of leadership? What advice would you give someone who was about to take on a leadership role?

PART II

The Tools

CHAPTER 3

People

"We all tend to think of our organizations as being more like machines than living systems," writes Peter Senge in *The Fifth Discipline*—and even when we don't consciously think of our organizations as machine-like, we nevertheless treat them as if they were.[1] One of my goals in this book is to change that, to encourage a serious reckoning with the fact that while our institutions too often feel to us like cold, mechanical entities, they are in fact made up of actual people and operate through the real interactions among them. There are two implications to understanding our institutions as living systems: first, that without the people they comprise and the people they serve, our institutions are hollow, useless structures; and second, that creating change within our institutions must be a people-centered act.

In part I of this book, as I discussed the transformation I hope to foster in our understanding of leadership in higher education, I talked a bit about why I focus on individuals as agents of change, a notion that may at first glance seem to contradict recent arguments about the systemic nature of power in contemporary culture. It is, without question, the institutions and systems holding sway over our lives that require transformation. These are the structures through which privilege and oppression are enacted and sustained, the structures that keep us ignorant of one another's struggles and keep us competing for resources and support.

These are the structures that must be reimagined and rebuilt in order to foster the kinds of generosity, equity, and integrity we'd like to see in the world. But those structures, understood as machines rather than living systems, come to possess a kind of impersonal, imperturbable inertia, the brick wall that not only foils all attempts at change but, as Sara Ahmed describes, has the potential to cause grievous harm to those who bash themselves against it.[2] That's certainly how many of us experience them. And those structures are not going to transform themselves; they are all too self-reinforcing.

Changing our institutions is going to require reframing our perspective around people, in two regards: one, we must recognize that the people within them keep the institutions going, and two, we need to find the people willing to plan, execute, and follow through on the work of transformation. The initiative for that work—the leadership that makes it possible—requires people, acting as individuals and building the coalitions and communities that can create something new.

And that leads me to this key claim: those people and coalitions and communities are far more important to cultivate and nurture than any of the other structures and processes and functions that make up our institutions. The relationships they foster and represent are the source of our institutions' humanity, and without them, even the most ostensibly mission-driven nonprofit may as well be a soulless private equity firm. None of our structures and processes matter at all unless they are at the service of people rather than the other way around.

In the open review of this book's draft, Martin Eve asked me a crucial question about the "temporality of universities," as he put it. Most of our institutions have been around for decades, and many even for centuries, and thus the argument that they are at the service of people opens a thorny question: "*which* people are to be served by the institution? The current faculty and students? Future faculty and students? The legacy of past faculty and students?"[3] Surely all of these people have some claim on the institution. I am willing to say that the past must loosen its grip on the present and future, but the struggle between present and future is acute. On the one hand, we are surrounded by the disastrous effects of contemporary organizations that operate as if there were no future to which we are obligated; climate change is perhaps the direst among the impacts of such presentism. On the other hand, we can also see around us institutions whose focus on the future—the future of shareholder value, for instance—allows them to avoid a full reckoning with the damage they're doing to their own employees today. Many universities operate in that latter space: endowed for the future but operating within the logic of scarcity in the present and thus requiring faculty and staff to sacrifice their own futures in service to some greater good that doesn't include them.

Generous leadership must place people first, and it must reckon directly with the difficulties of balancing the claims of the people who today sustain the institution and the people who tomorrow will benefit from it. Maintaining such a balance requires careful management, including the appropriate budgetary measures and governance structures and personnel policies that can ensure the institution's future. And of course one requirement for managing an organization well is a willingness to make hard choices when they are necessary for the organization's survival. But as Johnathan Nightingale and Melissa Nightingale—founders of the leadership training organization Raw Signal Group—note in their book *Unmanageable*, those choices are often predicated on several bad assumptions:

We're being asked as bosses to make choices between the
well-being of the communities we live in and the company we
help run. In almost every case, the idea that those things are
in conflict is a lie. We should all refuse to play that game. But
in the cases where they are in conflict, or where we're forced
to pretend that they are, we have a choice to make. *You* have a
choice to make. Companies don't have intrinsic value. People
do. Choose people.[4]

Of course, as Rebecca Kennison reminds me, it's not unusual
to suggest that some kinds of organizations *do* have intrinsic value
because of the good they seek to create in the world.[5] Institutions
of higher education and other public-service-oriented nonprofits
number among them. Nearly all such organizations—and even
a significant percentage of for-profit companies—would claim
to put people first, but in so doing they are most often pointing
outward, to the people they serve, rather than the people who do
the serving. Where they focus inward, they often do so by reducing the human from noun to adjective—*human resources, human
capital*—making clear the subjugation of people to their economic
function. Moreover, those of us who work for public-service organizations and institutions are imagined to do so because we have
some kind of calling that prioritizes the good of others over more
material or individual rewards; and as a result, when there are
difficult choices to be made, we are called upon to sacrifice.

This is the pattern that Fobazi Ettarh has called "vocational
awe," a set of beliefs that places some institutions (in Ettarh's case,
libraries) beyond critique, that turns labor on their behalf into
a "sacred calling," and that therefore justifies any damage done
to the lives of those who do the labor.[6] But the damage done by
turning labor into a vocation is real, and it manifests in massive

burnout and other forms of material, bodily, and psychological suffering in employees who internalize the belief that any form of complaint can threaten the organization's mission.[7]

Perhaps one part of the problem is right there in that term: *mission*. Universities and other nonprofit organizations, as well as public-service corporations, often aspire to be "mission-driven," without fully considering the lingering religious colonialism of the term. If we have a mission, who is it we're saving and at what expense to them, and to ourselves?

The project that I lead, Humanities Commons, has at times been described as "mission-driven," so I've been sitting with that term of late and trying to determine what I meant when I said it and whether there's a way to articulate the good it seeks to evoke without the echoes of domination it brings along. My colleagues and I talk a lot about "purpose" as a result, which maintains the goal while shedding some of the zeal. And as I'll discuss later, we also focus on being "values-enacted," keeping the shared principles from which we work centrally in view.

Beyond rejecting the colonialist implications, making a shift from "mission" to "values" reminds us that we can only serve the external purpose that we seek if we maintain an equal focus on the ways we work together within the organization. We cannot claim to be values-enacted in the work we're doing for others unless we bring those values to bear in all of our interactions with one another as well. As Madeline Shaw notes in *The Greater Good*, "to truly succeed as social entrepreneurs, we need to consider the integrity of our leadership practice as much as that of our product or service."[8] These internal interactions are often forgotten in the rush to do good in the external world.

When the Nightingales implore the bosses they advise to "choose people" over the companies the work for, they mean to remind us that the survival of an institutional structure—no matter how dedicated to the public good that structure may be— is not enough. For our institutions to do the good we want to see in the world, we have to care appropriately for the people that make up the institution. And in colleges and universities, those people are not just our present and future students but also the employees, the people without whom the institution would not function. There is no altruistic purpose that justifies sacrificing the basic humanity of people living today in order to keep the institution available for hypothetical people of tomorrow.

To put it plainly: Leadership requires leading *people* rather than leading *institutions*. It requires seeking at every turn to reframe your sense of purpose around the needs and concerns of those who make up the institution and do the work of pursuing its goals. It requires working to maintain a clear vision of the humanity not just of those whom the institution serves but also of the real humans behind the structures through which they are served. It's entirely too easy for the success of those structures to become the priority, to come to stand in for our purpose. Structural success can appear to be an end in itself, when in fact it is not—nor should be—anything more than a means for achieving our actual goals. Institutional soundness is significant enough; the instruments through which we work toward our purpose need to be healthy if we are to succeed. But elevating the health of the instruments above—or worse, *at the expense of*—the health of the people doing that work will not only undermine our purpose but is, in and of itself, inhumane.

Such inhumane focus was repeatedly demonstrated throughout the COVID-19 pandemic. A few university presidents early in 2020 publicly expressed their determination to reopen their institutions to in-person instruction as soon as they could, min-

imizing the potential risks for students and ignoring altogether
the dangers to staff, to faculty, and to their families and communities. Calls to return to instruction as usual were frequently framed
as a matter of concern for students and their futures: in order to
deliver the high-quality educational experience *they* deserve, *we*
must do whatever is necessary. One sees this, for instance, in a
message from Mitch Daniels, then president of Purdue University, to his university's community in April 2020, one month into
what became a multiyear pandemic:

> Closing down our entire society, including our university, was
> a correct and necessary step. It has had invaluable results. But
> like any action so drastic, it has come at extraordinary costs,
> as much human as economic, and at some point, clearly before
> next fall, those will begin to vastly outweigh the benefits of its
> continuance. Interrupting and postponing the education of
> tomorrow's leaders for another entire semester or year, is one of
> many such costs. So is permanently damaging the careers and
> lives of those who have made teaching and research their life's
> work, and those who support them in that endeavor.[9]

It's hard to remember in the worry over "the education of tomorrow's leaders," not to mention the not-so-veiled threat of injury
to faculty and staff's livelihoods, that the "benefits" of continuing
remote operations were primarily *fewer people dying.*

By contrast, consider the message sent in September 2020 by
Timothy White, the chancellor of the California State University
system, announcing the intent to continue virtual instruction
into early 2021. This decision was cast as "the only responsible
one available to us at this time," given "the twin North Stars of
safeguarding the health, safety and well-being of our faculty, staff,
students and communities, as well as enabling degree progression

for the largest number of students."[10] That the health and safety of those working to enable degree progression comes first here is not at all incidental. Contrast that with Daniels's message, in which the focus is on the costs of shutdown. Those costs are entirely external, derived from the sense that if we don't deliver the education our students are paying for—an education, I want to emphasize, that *everyone involved would agree* benefits from being delivered in person rather than remotely—those students will go elsewhere, and our institution will not survive.

I want to be clear here: I am a deep believer in the purpose of institutions of higher education and especially of broadly public-serving institutions of higher education, which have long functioned, if with deep flaws, as engines for social mobility, for empowerment, for democracy. Maintaining those engines is vital, and I, like the vast majority of faculty and staff, will do a lot to ensure that our institutions survive.[11] But institutions do not automatically *deserve* to survive based on that purpose alone and particularly not when it becomes evident that they will sacrifice the health and well-being of the people they comprise in order to do so.

Contrast this moral imperative with the charge borne by the executive teams at our colleges and universities. They have been charged by their boards with ensuring their institutions' survival, and a significant portion of that survival is bound up in the revenue provided by students who pay to attend. The primacy of that charge is exactly the problem: getting students on campus is a far more significant marker of "success" than their well-being once they've arrived, and certainly more than the well-being of those who fall on the expense side of the budget.[12] (There's another book to be written on this particular problem: the long-term ramifications of the neoliberal turn away from public investment in higher education, and toward a market-oriented model of financing and a corporate-derived board structure, which has inducted our campuses in the death cult of late capitalism.) The bottom line—and I use the term advisedly—is that we must consider how our institutions could possibly serve the people who learn in them if not for the people who teach in them and the people who build them and keep them operational. The relationship between an institution and those people is a key determinant of the institution's value, and if the lives of its employees do not come first, the institution's survival is moot.

What's more, caring for the lives of those employees means caring for their whole lives, and not just during the hours they spend on our campuses. This requires understanding that their families and communities are more than just background activity that sometimes inconveniently distracts the employees from their on-campus roles; these relations are, on the contrary, a key reason why employees fulfill their roles. As well, it requires backing that understanding up with family- and community-friendly policies that enable faculty and staff to meet the full range of their obligations. It requires a kind of care that is transitive, that doesn't just express concern for those directly connected with the campus but that also supports those people in caring for their objects of concern.

Caring for the entirety of these people's lives also means working to understand their differences and to support them in those differences. It means hearing and valuing their perspectives, *especially* when they disagree, rather than requiring that they get in line. Leading people can never mean simply ordering them about; instead it must be focused on building a collective sense of purpose and on finding ways to help everyone work toward living out that purpose. The collectivity of that purpose means, moreover, that sometimes you'll find yourself serving purposes that belong to the people you hope to lead. I'll talk about this more much later, but this kind of solidarity—understanding that those you lead can only be with you if they are certain that you are also with them—is a crucial component of living up to the purposes and values that our institutions espouse.

Questions for Reflection and Discussion

- What are the aspects of your job that are about management? What are the aspects that are about leadership? How are they related, and how are they distinct?

- What groups of people do you have the opportunity to build a kind of leadership among? What are their needs, and how can you help support them?

- Where do you feel conflict between your role as a manager and your role as a leader? How can those roles be brought into better alignment?

- How can you find ways to connect with and better understand the people you lead as *people*, rather than as functional units in your organization? How might your leadership practices expand to understand the full lives of those people?

CHAPTER 4

Yourself

Ari Weinzweig is the cofounder and CEO of Zingerman's. What began in 1982 as a small neighborhood deli in Ann Arbor, Michigan, has expanded over 40 years into what is now referred to as the Zingerman's Community of Businesses (or ZCoB, pronounced "zee-cob"), with over 500 employees and $50 million in annual sales. The ZCoB remains rooted in Ann Arbor despite its world-spanning influence. The businesses grew in no small part due to Weinzweig and his partners' unusual approach to managing them, which he describes as "anarcho-capitalism," or a mode of doing business "without getting hung up on hierarchy."[1] The ZCoB's influence has grown because of the ways they have documented and shared that approach. They built on the processes they developed for training new staff members, for instance, and created a suite of leadership seminars offered by ZingTrain. They also developed and published a series of leadership pamphlets and textbooks through Zingerman's Press.

I attended a ZingTrain master class in March 2022 and came away brimming with inspiration, thinking about ways that I could guide the team I was building for Humanities Commons through visioning exercises that would help us imagine the future we wanted to create and then chart our path toward it, about ways that I could use the principles of open book management to develop a greater sense of participant ownership of my community-oriented projects, and more. Perhaps the most important takeaway from the readings and class discussions for me, however, was a short passage in Weinzweig's essay "Twelve Tenets of Anarcho-Capitalism": "the best leaders are almost always the people who work hard on themselves. They treat themselves as they'd like to be treated by others, are the most self-reflective, and consistently work for meaningful self-improvement."[2]

This idea stopped me in my tracks, for a few reasons. Most notably, it suggested that the first object of leadership isn't *other* people but rather the self. Myself. Yourself.

It made sense to get this advice in the context of a leadership seminar: there I was, doing the work. But extrapolating that advice outward made it clear to me that the work of self-improvement shouldn't stop when the seminar was complete. There is always something more to learn, something more to think through, something more to change.

The best leaders, in doing this ongoing work of what might be understood as professional or personal development, hold themselves accountable to the same standards to which they hold others. They are willing to take up the same responsibilities, the same practices, the same structures that they create for their teams. In fact, good leaders understand themselves as being *part* of the team, rather than as guiding it from above. I might reverse a bit of Weinzweig's description by saying that leaders need to treat others with the same concern and compassion with which they'd like to be treated. But they also need to treat themselves in the same ways they'd treat their teams: with the same encouragement, the same guidance, the same requests, the same accountability.

All of us have seen any number of academic leaders (much less business or political leaders) who are happy to talk publicly about values such as equity, community, and compassion but whose behavior behind closed doors does not live up to those values. You may think immediately of the most obvious cases, leaders whose private failures of ethics led to public disgrace, sudden resignation, and institutional trauma. Michigan State has experienced an outsized share of this in recent years.

But there are less-obvious cases in which we live with the discrepancy between the ways some leaders talk about values and the ways they enact them. They might just be terrible bosses, making impossible demands of the members of their teams, failing to support them in reaching their personal and professional goals, belittling and chastising them, taking credit for their work, and more. These are the kinds of misbehaviors that too often go unremarked; as long as the leader in question appears to be getting things done, their damaging interactions within their teams are often swept aside. (And worse: as Katina Rogers reminds me, these are the people we too often see "fail up" across today's culture, wreaking havoc in organization after organization while steadily moving into positions of greater power and influence.[3]) The result, of course, is that many leaders do not recognize the gap between their public arguments and their private actions. What's more, any narcissistic tendencies they may have might allow them to believe that, because they are who they are, their actions cannot be wrong.

Breaking through those failures of self-recognition can be painful, but it's a necessary first step to developing better leadership practices. Because here's the thing: even if you can't see the distance between your words and your actions, those around you can. James Baldwin made the point by quoting a song: "I can't believe what you say ... because I see what you do."[4] Until you've fully reckoned, for instance, with the ways that social and institutional hierarchies permit you to excel at others' expense—or more simply with the ways that your actions and energies affect those around you—you can't really be up to the task of making a better workplace, much less a better world.

So: be the change. It's a cliché, for sure, but one with teeth. As Weinzweig notes, we have to be willing to "work for meaningful self-improvement" if we're going to be capable of making any improvements in the world around us. "Meaningful" is not just a throwaway modifier here; self-improvement requires work—but what kind of work? Not necessarily therapy, though there are worse places to begin. The benefit of therapy (says the total non-therapist, so apply that disclaimer to my statement) may come less from the actual advice or intervention delivered by the therapist and more from your own commitment to introspection: to consider your behaviors, your reactions, your habits, your defenses from a new perspective. That perspective can be gained in any number of ways, if you're willing to take it seriously and to work for it. It can come from deep reading and contemplation. It can come from journaling or other forms of creative production. It can come from spiritual practices, including meditation and prayer. It can come from engaging seriously with the kind of 360-degree review that asks not just your supervisor but also your colleagues and your direct reports for feedback.

The second step, as Rebecca Kennison reminds me, is to *act on* the knowledge this self-examination provides.[5] This translation of knowledge into action isn't easy. It's deeply failure-prone, and it requires a willingness to begin again and again. I hope that the chapters that follow provide some support in doing so.

Part of what Weinzweig is getting at in his assertion that the best leaders are the ones who *consistently* work hard on themselves is that becoming a person who can lead well is a process without end, one that cannot ever be completed. There isn't a credential offered upon successful conclusion of a program of self-improvement, entitling you to operate as a Certified Good Leader. Rather, this kind of internal reckoning with your engagements with the world, and with the people around you, will—and should—be part of the rest of your life. Take it seriously.

Questions for Reflection and Discussion

- What practices do you regularly engage in that might lead you to the kinds of "meaningful self-improvement" that Weinzweig argues could make you a better leader? What practices do you resist? Why?

- How would you describe the best boss you've ever had? The worst boss? What have you learned to emulate from the best? What have you learned to avoid from the worst?

- What do you think you could learn in order to help you create the kind of working environment you'd like to be part of? How might you go about learning it?

CHAPTER 5

Vulnerability

In the interviews I conducted with academic leaders, many of them related difficult moments at which they had faced the displeasure of the people with whom they work. (Deans, I add, seem to do a *lot* of this.) All of these leaders, in various ways, shared a common mantra: "It's not about you."

This mantra carries a number of reminders that are important for engaging in forms of leadership from the positional to the grassroots. Many of the folks I talked to who used this phrase were seeking ways to bear up while they faced public criticism and even anger. "It's not about you" was for them a means of holding off the reflexive tendency to become defensive or even angry in return by recognizing that, however personal the criticism may have felt in the moment, it was driven by the situation, the structure, the role. "It's not about you" calls forth an internal equanimity that can allow a leader under fire to focus on hearing and understanding the substance of what's being said, rather than shielding themselves from the emotion that surrounds the message. "It's not about you" is also a reminder to decenter the self in favor of a collective good; as Evviva Weinraub Lajoie told me, "you need to think about the best interests of the community, of the project, of the institution, and so you have to check your ego at the door."[1]

Checking your ego is not always easy, but the approach to leadership for which I am advocating—focusing on bringing people together and building coalitions to enact transformative change—requires a willingness to do what's necessary to get beyond self-interest. One key form of self-interest is self-protection, the desire to avoid discomfort. But change and discomfort go hand in hand; as Edgar and Peter Schein note in *Humble Inquiry*, allowing oneself to be unsettled is a key aspect of the learning process necessary to building a better institution. They encourage leaders to ask deep questions of those around them and to put their own assumptions aside in favor of potentially unexpected answers: "when you genuinely ask, you temporarily empower the other person in the conversation and make yourself vulnerable, for a time. You have also opened the door to the possibility of deepening a relationship."[2] Opening oneself to what others are saying entails lowering the protective barriers of ego, along with experience and privilege, in order to let other perspectives take precedence.

The knowledge gained and connections developed when these barriers are down can be extraordinary, but lowering them also creates the possibility of being on the receiving end of criticism and even anger. Lots of us experience deep fear in the face of others' anger—many women in particular are terrified of the potential, if often imagined, violence that could lie behind male rage[3]—and giving that anger room for expression requires a form of equanimity that can be hard to muster. But there's a difference between developing that equanimity and being unaffected by others' emotional responses: equanimity opens space for deepened understanding, but it requires vulnerability, and without a willingness to be vulnerable, understanding becomes impossible.

There is a kind of leader—particularly one in a highly visible position, likely to have been trained in traditional styles of management that privilege the tough figure who speaks firmly and decisively from a position of authority—who may worry that the apparent passivity and openness implied in deep listening will set them up to appear "weak." This concern stems especially from the emotional responses that such listening may evoke: for a leader to reveal their unease, sorrow, uncertainty, or regret may feel too much like showing their belly. They may feel overexposed and vulnerable to attack.

Yes, they will be vulnerable, certainly—but vulnerability does not imply weakness. In fact, the association of vulnerability with weakness is part of the problem that we face across many areas of public life today. Leaders, we have long been told, are supposed to be firm and forthright. Decisive. Respected. Looked up to—and therefore elevated above the crowd. This remove grants them protection, but it also creates distance. If you think about leadership as grounded in relationship-building and connection, however, you'll begin to recognize that our leaders need to come down from the dais in order to reach the people with whom they need to work. This is not weakness, yet it does require a willingness to make oneself vulnerable.

If vulnerability is not weakness, then what is it? Brené Brown has described vulnerability as "having the courage to show up when you can't control the outcome."[4] In fact, it's letting go of the need to control the outcome. It's a willingness to engage directly with the people in your institution and the people that your institution serves, both those who agree and those who disagree, and to imagine what you might do together. Vulnerability is a willingness to try ideas out and a readiness to acknowledge when your ideas are wrong. Vulnerability is an admission that you are human and that your knowledge is partial.

The best teachers reveal this kind of vulnerability all the time; as Eric Elliott told me, "The faculty members who connect most with their students are willing to go into a state of vulnerability within the classroom to field questions that might make some other faculty members shiver." For Elliott, these questions are often personal: teaching at a community college in "deep, deep Louisiana" means that his students frequently face a range of life circumstances that he can provide perspective on given his own experience, when, that is, he's willing to share it with them.[5] But vulnerability in the classroom need not be about the personal; as a graduate student whom I interviewed told me, "it was a real exercise in vulnerability for me to have a student ask me a question, and to stew for a second and then just come right out and say 'you know what, I don't know, but I'm going to write that down.'"[6] Revealing to a classroom full of students that you need to investigate a question before providing an answer is an exercise in vulnerability. The same is true of revealing that you need the input and support of the people around you in order to make the best decisions you can.

Vulnerability is thus complexly intertwined with humility; in fact, vulnerability might accurately be described as the way that humility feels from the inside. As Sarah Buss notes, "to be humble is to appreciate one's fallibility. It is to know how little one knows. . . . And it involves being disposed to learn what one can from [other] people. To be humble is to appreciate that when one disagrees with someone, it may not be this other person who is confused and mistaken."[7] In fact, as Sonja Fritzsche remarks, "Disagreement is an opportunity to ask exploratory questions to understand more why someone came to their conclusion."[8] Asking those questions requires the ability to consider—even, as Buss says, *appreciate*—that you just might be wrong, which is in turn a willingness to make yourself vulnerable.

In doing this, you might begin to grasp why vulnerability's apparent opposite—invulnerability—is not merely impossible to achieve but also undesirable. Invulnerability isn't strength. However much leaders might be encouraged, or encourage themselves, to "grow a thicker skin," armoring yourself against criticism is counterproductive. On the one hand, you do need to have the internal resources that make it possible to sit with and listen to criticism, and "thicker skin" might be a useful metaphor for describing those resources. On the other hand, a thicker skin might also be a way of deflecting blows or fending off an entirely human reaction to them. As Dianne Harris recalled, after she was once told during a crisis that she needed grow a thicker skin, having thought to herself, "why wouldn't I want to feel this?"[9]

Armor-plated leaders might be protected from being hurt, but they're also prevented from interacting with their environment, from sensing change, from connecting. Engaged leadership in fact requires vulnerability: removing the armor, grappling with difficulties, experiencing changes in the environment, and accepting criticism. Only through such willingness to be vulnerable—by having the courage to show up unarmored—can that engagement produce the learning and the relationships necessary to moving an institution in a better direction.

This is never truer than in times of crisis. When your community is frightened or hurting, it's crucial to be with them not just in your rhetoric but in your actions too: to acknowledge and honor their fear and pain as well as your own. This is risky to do. If you haven't earned the trust of your community, it's easy for public expressions like this to sound like a calculated and empty form of faux empathy, of the "I feel your pain" variety. And this leads us back to the question that goaded me toward this book: How can you enact generosity in hard times? In no small part the answer requires having built the foundations of generosity before times get hard, by having established the generous principles and practices that build trust and then relying on those principles and practices to help get you through.

If you have that trust, you can build on it by sharing your own concerns with your community. But if you haven't yet built that trust? *Acknowledging that*, admitting mistakes, and expressing your genuine desire to repair the breach can begin the process. (I'll talk more about trust ahead.)

The key here is recognizing which concerns of your community in crisis are ones you genuinely share and which are ones you don't share but need to understand. This is especially true when those concerns are *about you* and your willingness and ability to work through the crisis with your community rather than at their expense. When your institution or your team is looking to you for solutions, it's vitally important to share not just what you do know but what you don't, what you need their help with, where pockets of uncertainty make clear answers difficult. And it's especially important to remain in open communication; this communication should not become a one-way transmission of announcements and updates but should be an opportunity for dialogue.

I've had experiences with leaders who are good at this kind of openness, and—as the earlier chapter on crisis might suggest—I've had experiences with leaders who are disastrously bad at it. Far too many of us have known a university president who effectively built walls around the office, using an inner circle of advisors to keep others away. In my interview with him, Benjamin Lowenkron pointedly characterized the upper administration at his institution as the "C-suite," which marks both their remove from the work being done on the ground and the enclosure that protects them.[10] Directives and pronouncements emanate from such a C-suite, but crucial information that upper administrators need to know may never reach them. Worse, they may receive that information without being required to acknowledge or act upon it. Worst of all, the distinction between those two circumstances—between engineered ignorance and willful ignoring—is invisible to the community, which is left to deal with the consequences alone. As a result, rumors spread unchecked and discontent festers.

On the other hand, I've worked with some phenomenal leaders, and I hope that you have as well, leaders who can provide models for the kinds of openness and vulnerability we should all work toward. For the last several years I've worked directly with a dean who, as the horrors inflicted by Larry Nassar at MSU were revealed on the national stage, spoke openly and honestly enough with the university that we could see his emotional response and understand he was experiencing the same turmoil we were and, moreover, that he would work with us to forge a new path. That ethical, *human* presence in a traumatic moment was personally risky, but it inspired the trust necessary for creating change both in response to these events and in other areas. I'll share more about those changes ahead, but for now it's crucial to note that they required the risks involved in frank communication.

Frank communication is of course not a one-way process; a person in a position of leadership has to be willing not just to share their own emotional responses but also to create space for the responses of others. As Heifetz and Laurie argue, this disposition to listen to "voices of leadership from below" is "the foundation of an organization that is willing to experiment and learn." Those voices are often airing crucial forms of dissent that can surface new ideas. "But, in fact," they write, "whistle-blowers, creative deviants, and other such original voices routinely get smashed and silenced in organizational life. They generate disequilibrium, and the easiest way for an organization to restore equilibrium is to neutralize those voices, sometimes in the name of teamwork and 'alignment.'"[11] Squashing the dissent squashes the new ideas, and while the consensus implied in "alignment" might be desirable, manufactured consent will ultimately create growing misalignment, as resistance and distrust fester.

This is not to say that all dissent is the same. Nearly any academic will recognize the degree to which one loud, usually entitled voice can dominate and derail a meeting, or a classroom, such that no productive exchange is possible. As Robin Schulze shared with me, there comes a time when a dean, for instance, has to be willing to face the difficult act of saying "enough" to the toxic voices. This in itself is a vulnerable moment, because, as she noted, "you will be accused of everything." Yet, she went on to say, the cost of not interrupting the toxicity of those who derail productive communication is too great: "We have to realize that everybody who's doing this, they're not just doing it to us, they're doing it to all their colleagues, and it feels exactly the same way for all their colleagues"; if there seems to be something "more important than doing something about it—there probably isn't, because these are fragile ecosystems, these academic departments and the culture that you create."[12]

It remains crucial, however, to distinguish between the truly toxic and the productively critical; shutting down the former can be necessary to the functioning of a community, while shutting down the latter can cause the community to disintegrate. It's often difficult to tell them apart, particularly when, as Dorothea Salo points out, the toxicity has developed in response to more productive forms of criticism being ignored.[13] Accurately judging that distinction, and figuring out whether it's possible to get the toxic individual onto a better path, requires some careful soul-searching and discernment. Is what's at stake genuinely collective, or is it just ego? This kind of judgment may require external support, provided through conversations with what Arthur Costa and Bena Kallick have defined as a "critical friend . . . a trusted person who asks provocative questions, provides data to be examined through another lens, and offers critique of a person's work as a friend."[14] A critical friend can help you see what ego won't allow you to recognize and can provide a safe environment in which to begin the process of removing your armor.

A key goal is developing institutions in which we can all be critical friends to one another. Getting there, however, means beginning somewhere, and that beginning requires being willing to take on a bit of risk. There is risk involved in coalition building, in opening up decision-making processes, in inviting critique, in remaining open to ongoing communication. And there are certainly risks involved in allowing those you work with to see your own uncertainty, your frustration, your anxiety. But *not* doing so presents guaranteed problems: invulnerability breeds communication failures and active distrust. Acknowledging and revealing your vulnerability can be painful, but it creates the possibility for real trust and communication to grow.

One word of caution, though: few things are more infuriating than the *performance* of vulnerability. Wearing your worries on your sleeve can wind up looking like a transparent attempt to fend off criticism through an appeal to sympathy. Genuine vulnerability is not about display but is rather about being wholly present in a difficult situation, opening up real communication, and inviting participation in thinking through solutions. It also requires follow-through: keeping the lines of communication open once decisions have been made, ensuring that the reasoning that went into the decisions is in line with the values your community upholds. Not everyone will agree with those decisions, but your willingness to show up, to accept criticism, and to hear new ideas can help maintain trust in difficult times.

Questions for Reflection and Discussion

- In your role as a leader, how do you find yourself attempting to be invulnerable? What habits or structures of self-protection have you built? What would you need in order to let go of those habits or structures while managing your own fear?

- How can you practice vulnerability with those you lead? How can you let your community in on your processes and challenges in ways that might help build greater understanding and trust?

- In what situations does the team you lead need to hear more about what you are thinking and feeling? In what situations do you need to make room to hear more from them?

CHAPTER 6

Together

"The leadership skills for the future of higher education are 100% coalition-building and relationships."[1]

This cut-to-the-chase assertion came to me from Chris Bourg, director of libraries at MIT. In our interview, Chris talked about the ways she'd built relationships with the libraries' staff, the upper administration, the MIT faculty, and the libraries' visiting committee (an MIT governance structure that acts as an ongoing external review team) in order to create the MIT Framework. This framework promised to transform MIT's negotiations with large corporate publishers, but far more importantly, it was offered to the broader network of research libraries in the interest of transforming publisher relations in librarianship. At the time of our interview, the framework had received more than 200 endorsements from libraries and library organizations across the country, creating a powerful coalition for real, material change.[2]

Coalition-building and relationships form the heart of generous leadership, and I'm grateful to the many folks I talked with who, like Chris, emphasized that point for me. When I first began working on this project, my focus, and the primary subject pronoun I relied on, was "you." I felt that my argument needed to be addressed to you, the reader, so as to focus on your role as a potential leader, whether or not that leadership derived from a position of authority. I still believe that all transformative change must start with you: without your determination to make things better, and your commitment to the work ahead, there can be only more of the same.

As readers began to respond to my early blog posts about this project, however, it became clear that addressing *you* left something out: as crucial as you are to the process of creating transformative change, the key pronoun for thinking about the future of our institutions is not "you" but rather "us." This "us" is not a configuration that exists naturally, though, except in some limited, and often limiting, senses. Our notions of "us" commonly develop out of our lived experience and so come to be associated with "people like me," thus excluding more members of our institutions than they include. To make real change in our institutions and in the world, we have to work toward an "us" that is expansive and responsive, an "us" that embraces difference and reaches out to build and maintain the connections that can create not just collectives, but coalitions.

So, as a result of the conversations I had with leaders like Chris, my focus shifted to exploring how we build the path from "you" to "us"—the process of connecting and developing the relationships that will allow all of us to work together on making the more just, more resilient, more caring institutions we need.

Building resilient, collaborative, equity-minded teams has turned out to be a significant part of my work. When I became the director of Digital Humanities at Michigan State, I was tasked with helping a dispersed group of folks working in campus centers, labs, and projects across the university figure out how to work together to become something more than the sum of their parts. I frequently joke that I was given neither carrots nor sticks to make this collaboration happen; I had a tiny budget to work with, and I had no authority over the units that I was trying to bring together. To the extent we've been successful, DH@MSU has grown through cultivating relationships and developing shared governance processes that can help support all of our work.

I've done similar work as the director of Humanities Commons. We founded the project while I was a member of the senior team of the Modern Language Association, and I brought it with me when I moved to MSU. Since that time, thanks to significant external grant support and an equal measure of internal relationship building, I've been able to expand the project team to include 14 people with various percentages of time commitment to the project. This team is geographically dispersed, with members in Michigan, New York, Toronto, Montreal, and Thessaloniki (!), and its members bring a wide range of skill sets and backgrounds to the project. We've grounded our work together through a careful process of developing a statement of shared values, articulating our shared purpose, developing our shared vision, and translating all of that into ways of collaborating in the day-to-day to achieve our farthest-reaching goals.

Likewise, as president of the board of directors of the Educopia Institute, I've worked closely with the staff to help guide the organization through a momentous leadership transition. Educopia's founder, Katherine Skinner, had served as executive director for more than a decade, but, as I'll describe in greater detail when I tell Educopia's story, she had come to recognize that the organization's future success required that she make way for new leadership. The multiyear transition began with Katherine cultivating leadership potential within Educopia's staff and continued through a facilitated process of board development. In the course of our work together, the board came to the decision that it was time to implement a new model of shared leadership, with three codirectors supported through a collaborative relationship with the board.

Each of these experiences has required a deep commitment to working together, especially when collaborative processes demand slower forward movement. And each of these experiences has deepened my conviction that sharing power is the key to undoing the toxic model of leadership explored in the first part of this book. That model is entirely focused on the power of the individual and on the assumption that the individual's reach becomes greater as they climb the org chart. Of course, power does grow in that direction: with the elevation produced by promotion comes an expansion in one's sphere of influence and institutional authority. But what else often happens is that the connections available to the position narrow, until you find yourself at the pinnacle of the institution: you're at the center of power, yet you're sitting there alone. Success in such a leadership role—in any leadership role, really, whether one labeled such by the institution or one emerging from a grassroots project—requires developing the relationships that can sustain the work.

The necessity of those relationships becomes most visible when the typically pyramid-shaped org chart is flipped in order to represent not authority but responsibility instead. As Matthew Caiazza notes, the resulting stakeholder responsibility chart, which emphasizes servant leadership, demonstrates that the singular top executive in fact has the entire pyramid teetering *on them*; they bear the impossible weight of the organization and its expectations alone.[3]

At an institution the size of MSU, that weight numbers into the hundreds of thousands of people: not just the more than 14,000 employees but the 55,000 current students and their families as well. And then there are the alumni, the contractors, and the surrounding community. With all of that responsibility resting on the shoulders of one human, it's not hard to understand

STAKEHOLDER RESPONSIBILITY CHART

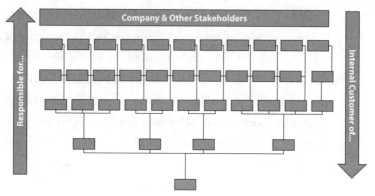

Matthew Caiazza, "So You Want to Climb the Org Chart," *Medium*, March 30, 2020, https://mcaiazza.medium.com/so-you-want-to-climb-the-org-chart-ffb1e9bb02d9

why the turnover rate for college and university presidents has become so high.

As my colleagues on the board and staff of the Educopia Institute came to realize, a traditional search for a new executive director with all the skills, knowledge, and relationships necessary to lead a values-enacted organization into the future might have been successful, but it might also have set that new leader up for failure. Opting for a shared leadership model enabled us to broaden the base on which the organization's responsibilities rest, by creating a team of leaders whose skills complement one another. Shared leadership also minimizes the risk involved in future leadership turnover, as seeking a new member to join the leadership team will open more new possibilities than would another costly search to replace the chief executive for, perhaps, only the short term.

Not every institution or organization is prepared to move to

VERTICAL VERSUS SHARED LEADERSHIP

Vertical leadership   Shared leadership

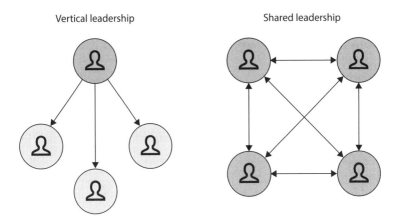

"Shared Leadership," Valamis, updated March 22, 2023, https://www.valamis.com/hub
/shared-leadership

a fully shared leadership model, which would replace the chief executive with a truly collaborative team committed to collective decision-making, though I strongly believe that many of them would benefit from that model. But all organizations, from the smallest nonprofits to the largest global universities, must focus more on strengthening the bonds across the org chart than on building the strength of the individuals who occupy the boxes. Those bonds are the relationships necessary to ensuring that the structure as a whole will stand, and the more that power is shared within an organization, the more significant the relationships become.[4]

Frederic Laloux argues, in fact, that thinking about power as something that inheres in some positions and not in others, and that those in other positions have to be *empowered*, is part of the problem. Empowerment, he notes, "means that someone at the top must be wise or noble enough to give away some of his power." Instead, he asks us to consider what might happen "if power weren't a zero-sum game? What if we could create organizational structures and practices that didn't need empowerment because, by design, everybody was powerful and no one powerless?"[5]

An environment such as this, in which everyone is powerful, demands a willingness in each individual to decenter the demands of the self and instead recognize the mutuality required for connection. As Sarah Buss notes in the introduction to *Radical Humility*, "retreating from the center of things—both in reality and in one's self-conception—is inseparable from forging connections that expand the boundaries of one's self."[6] In other words, it's through connections that we become larger, not through ego. Building connections requires stepping out of the center— whether that centrality comes from being the boss or from being in a culturally dominant position or from some other aspect of self-conception—and working instead on building a coalition, while continuing to account for the influence of power dynamics in organizational life. We need to build coalitions in order to transform complex organizations, and we need to act in solidarity, with an awareness of the movement of power so that those coalitions may succeed.

Most community-oriented organizations believe they understand that. And yet, as Katherine Skinner told me, she's always surprised by the number of communities that "push back when I say relationship-building is one of the things we need to be focusing on right now. 'Well, we've got relationships. We're doing just fine.' *Now* you may be doing just fine, but you better be feeding that all the time or you won't be anymore."[7] Even good relationships aren't static, and they aren't permanent; they need ongoing care to thrive.

Institutional structures often inhibit real community and relationship building, however. In one of the interviews I conducted for this volume, I put the question rather bluntly: given that many respondents I'd spoken with had noted the importance of coalition building—and that it was overwhelmingly the women leaders who had said so—with whom does the BIPOC female president of a small liberal arts college get to build a coalition? My respondent, a little bemused, replied first with "other presidents of small liberal arts colleges." She followed that, though, with a different kind of response, one focused on encouraging greater participation in leadership among her own faculty: "showing people what's in it for them" by helping them see their potential for real influence, now and in the future. "Every president has a 10-year expiration date on their back," she said. So, in addressing her faculty colleagues, she might ask, "do you want to be in the position in 10 years where you're the one who's calling the shots? . . . [I]f you do, then let me help you get there." She went on to note the idea "that politicians start campaigning for reelection the day after they get into office. I kind of think presidents need to start thinking about their exit strategies from the day they get into office. It's not just legacy. It's—what do you want to be possible that's not possible now?"[8]

What my respondent revealed in her comments is not just a recognition that positional power does not last forever or that an individual occupying a leadership role is never there more than temporarily. She also suggests that the most important goal for a leader should be working with others to help them take on leadership roles, thereby creating the possibility of a future where the institution can be better off than it is today.

Such a willingness to recognize one's own finitude is a profoundly ethical position. On the one hand, it stems from a deep acknowledgment that any position of structural leadership will of necessity come to an end, and so the best thing you can do for the work you want to accomplish is to enable that work to live on without you, to make opportunities for others to carry it forward. On the other hand, it comes from an equally deep acknowledgment that *you cannot do everything*, even while you're the one leading. You need others not just to help but to feel the same kind of ownership over the work that you feel.

There's a common aspect of leadership that often gets described in the literature as creating "alignment" with the leader's vision, and it sounds much like what I've just outlined: getting a team to buy in and carry out the work leading to a strategic goal. However, as Peter Senge notes, alignment operates as a coercive, top-down form of agenda setting: "Today, 'vision' is a familiar concept in corporate leadership. But when you look carefully you find that most 'visions' are one person's (or one group's) vision imposed on an organization. Such visions, at best, command compliance—not commitment. A shared vision is a vision that many people are truly committed to, because it reflects their own personal vision."[9] The gap between a leader's vision and a truly shared vision is what often makes strategic planning in our institutions feel like busy work, with an enormous amount of time and effort invested in arriving at predetermined conclusions. The vision for the future that such plans attempt to develop cannot work unless it's truly shared, and it can't be truly shared unless it's developed collectively.

A genuinely collective vision is one key to institutional transformation, but of course there's an enormous amount of work involved in bringing together the people required to develop that collective vision, much less to work together toward realizing it. Collective planning may not come naturally for leaders who've been steeped in conventional hierarchies and workflows, but a new generation of leaders is emerging today and bringing with them what Helen Berry described to me as "a new style" of leading for transformative change. Berry called this style "multinuclear leadership," noting that she has seen it used in community organizations and that it has often been adopted by women leaders within the academy.[10] This leadership style works to empower the entire community that will be affected by a decision, not by creating a single forum or feedback session in which the loudest voices can dominate but rather by organizing that community into working groups charged with particular tasks; these groups then share the work they've done with the community as a whole for discussion and review.

One of the conventional assumptions about decision-making, of course, is that collective processes like this are inevitably slower and that sometimes you just need some singular someone to be the decider. Perhaps. Unilateral decisions may well have more efficient arrival times. Those decisions, however, still have to be implemented, and the implementation of plans over which an entire community feels ownership will nearly always be more effective. (I provide an illustrative example in chapter 15, "Transforming Institutional Structure.") For this reason, as Dean Spade has explored, one of the most important foundations for mutual aid organizations is building the "efficient, participatory, transparent decision-making structures" that can "prevent the conflicts that tend to tear groups apart, divide participants from each other, and drive people away."[11] Building those structures takes time, but it is time well invested.

A process of collective decision-making, used in the context of strategic planning, has the potential to create shared ownership of the outcomes, but it can only if the positional leaders involved approach it with a truly open perspective. As Berry notes, this is not a "directive, top-down, here's my great vision" mode of operation; it's instead "facilitative . . . a bottom-up process." As such, it requires that those authorizing or organizing the process be willing to step out of the center and allow leadership to grow from multiple points within the community: "If what emerges is different in the process of doing that vision thing," Berry notes, "you have to be willing to change and shift your perspective."[12]

The response of some more traditionally oriented leaders to the processes of shared governance, and to the outcomes they produce, is often to say, "yes, but the staff doesn't have the big picture in mind" or "the faculty doesn't have access to the institutional knowledge that I have." If this statement is true, then the processes have become a form of window dressing for top-down decision-making. The first step in building distributed, collective planning or governance should be precisely to ensure that everyone involved has access to the big picture and all the forms of institutional knowledge that leadership requires. This means that a positional leader engaging in such a process has to be willing to share what they know and to make more visible what's often kept behind the scenes. I'll dig further into this when I talk about transparency, but for now it's important to note that it's only through principled determination to be open with the folks invested in the institution that real trust, and real relationships, can be built.

Those relationships are a prerequisite for shaping an institution's future together, but it's important not to overlook the human significance of the relationships in and of themselves. As Este Pope, a librarian at Amherst College and an active participant in multi-institutional collaborations, reminded me: just as important as "what we're accomplishing" is "that goodwill and being able to really delight in actual relationships with people. . . . This is modeling what—in whatever bigger framework—could be possible."[13]

Questions for Reflection and Discussion

- What relationships would be most important to your ability to create meaningful change in your institution or in your corner of your institution? How can you go about building those relationships?
- What coalitions can you imagine bringing together— across units, across fields, across employment categories, across other boundaries—to work toward the change you imagine? What would be required to create those connections?

CHAPTER 7

Trust

Transforming an organizational culture requires a deep trust among those working for change. The people engaged in such work need to feel that their concerns are safe with one another, to believe in one another's goodwill and commitment, and to know that the collective will support them in tricky moments. In a trusting community, people are able to experiment, to suggest new paths, to take risks. Without trust, they shut down. They stagnate, and their environment deteriorates.

I know this in large part because I've worked in deeply mistrustful environments in which, for instance, no one had confidence in how higher-ups would receive new ideas. These ideas were likely to be dismissed or ignored, or worse still, the people who ventured them could wind up publicly berated and humiliated. As a result, unsurprisingly, no one brought forward new ideas. Everyone felt vulnerable, and no one trusted the environment enough to inhabit that vulnerability. Communication among employees was reduced to what was strictly necessary and was starched with formality, but the back channels were filled with discontent. Morale was terrible; most everyone kept their heads down and did what they had to do, but almost no one was happy about it. Furthermore, no one could imagine any way to make it better.

I've also worked in environments in which everyone felt they had the room to think differently, to disagree, to propose significant changes to ways of working. Everyone knew their ideas would be soundly critiqued and might eventually be rejected, which at times generated nervousness and disappointment. Those feelings didn't generally escalate into withdrawal and resentment, however, as everyone had reason to be confident that their colleagues shared a common set of goals and values and that airing their disagreements in an open fashion could push them in a positive direction. In describing his own experiences in similar environments, Sayeed Choudhury said they often produced "a little bit of discomfort, in some cases maybe a lot of discomfort. But upon reflection, recognizing there was nothing mean or disrespectful ... about that conversation, and wow, it has actually given me a lot to think about. Those are the folks that I would build a web of connections with."[1] Environments like these are collegial in the deepest sense: rarely in full agreement, not always "nice," but bound together by a shared trust in one another's motives and a shared commitment to work toward something better.

Given this collegial alternative, an obvious question then surfaces: How can we build, maintain, and communicate trust within an organization? Unfortunately, there aren't any shortcuts. Building trust of the kind necessary for a functional, resilient, caring organization takes significant time and effort. There's no simple formula that can get you from the stifling environment I described to a supporting one.

There are a few seeds, though, that leaders in an organization can sow with their colleagues, seeds that must be cultivated consistently over time so that trust may take root. Moreover, the trust that is cultivated must be mutual: the members of a team need to trust those leading it, and our willingness to trust others depends heavily on our feeling trusted in return. It's too often true, as

Charles Feltman has argued, that in work environments characterized by mistrust, "the problem starts with the leader's lack of trust in the people who work for and with them."[2] As Frederic Laloux notes, when a manager doesn't trust the folks who work under them, they tend to "subject them to all sorts of controls, rules, and punishments," and as a result their employees "try to game the system," ultimately convincing the manager that they were right not to trust them. However, he argues, if you "[m]eet people with practices based on trust ... they will return your trust with responsible behavior."[3]

Because mutual mistrust is so pervasive, positional leaders who want to change their organization often have to root out and remediate the effects bred by those who preceded them. (I wish I had a dollar for every time I've heard a faculty member say, "the dean will never let us" or "the provost will insist," without recognizing that what led to this assumption was an event eight years old and two administrations ago.) The damage done in mistrustful environments is highly durable, and building and maintaining the trust that can heal the damage requires significant, focused effort to trust others, backed by a shared commitment to open communication and consistent follow-through.

Feltman's model of the often-unconscious choices that each of us makes about whether to trust another person involves "four distinct assessments" of that person's *care, sincerity, reliability*, and *competence*. In this model, the decision to trust someone depends on whether we believe that they share our concerns, that they mean what they say, that they will follow through on their promises, and that they are capable of succeeding. Distrust, by contrast, is characterized by the belief that "*what is important to me is not safe with this person.*"[4] As Feltman notes, the thing that does not feel safe can be anything: a position, a project, a personal value, or something as basic as health and well-being. Once that sense of safety is compromised, so too are the possibilities for mutual work toward institutional change.

All of the leaders I interviewed for this book mentioned the significance of trust in leadership, but only a few spoke explicitly about the work involved in building it. A college president mentioned the importance of demonstrating that you genuinely, authentically love what you do; that demonstration of care can help those around you trust your motives and your commitment.[5] Likewise, Robin Schulze noted that "you work people up to a level of trust by showing what you can do."[6] And Chris Long elaborated on the deep intertwining of care and reliability:

> When you are intentional about identifying the values you care about, and intentional about trying to put those values into practice in every decision you make, in every encounter you have, in every policy that you develop, in every bylaw you revise, and you're also honest with yourself and your colleagues when you fail—which you do all the time, almost every day, to live up to the values you say you care most deeply about, because there are multiple values that are always operating on us, even if we could live out our values in every context. Over time the roots and the shoots of trust begin to grow. And that's when my job as dean changed.[7]

The proof of the pudding, in other words, is in the eating: the alignment of words and actions, the demonstration of competence over time, and the consistent desire to operate from a values-enacted perspective are necessary elements of building trust. As Rebecca Kennison commented in the open review of this chapter, however, the cycle of mistrust is hard to break, and avoiding a retreat into reflexive back-channeling and suspicion requires "renewed, conscious commitment to enacting those shared values—through intentional daily practice."[8]

Demonstrating care, sincerity, reliability, and competence is important to developing trust at the individual level, but developing trust at the institutional level requires even more concentrated effort in building the systems and practices that can reinforce that trust. Trust requires a set of shared values, a shared commitment to those values, and a deep belief that the commitment is in fact shared. Some elements in establishing and reinforcing that commitment include the following.

Transparency. I discuss transparency in more detail in chapter 10, but for now it's important to note that the goal of transparency is to keep everyone fully informed about the circumstances that support and constrain decision-making, the principles and processes that will be used to make those decisions, and the outcomes after decisions are implemented. One important example of such transparency is open book finance, first explored by Jack Stack and Bo Burlingham in *The Great Game of Business*. Open book finance in the corporate context asks business leaders to fully educate their employees—not just the executives, and not just the finance department, but *all* of their employees—about the business's financial position, its metrics for success, and its means and constraints for achieving them. The "great game" part of Stack and Burlingham's model refers to what comes next: getting everyone involved in working toward the business's success by ensuring that everyone has a real, material stake in the outcome.[9] The idea of open book finance has been expanded by others, including my friends at Zingerman's, into "open book management," which applies the same principles to decision-making throughout the organization, keeping employees invested and involved in the organization's direction.

Transparency of this sort begins with opening up the black boxes of institutional operations, sharing the clearest possible picture of the institution's present state, the path ahead, and the work necessary to accomplishing institutional goals. The purpose of sharing that information, however, is not simply to say that you have done so but to seek the active involvement of those who make up the institution in achieving its ends. Stack and Burlingham note, somewhat optimistically, that "[b]ecause you have trusted individuals with the information, they feel a commitment and a sense of ownership to act on it." But they go on to point out the absolute certainty of the contrary: "Why would people commit to action or making a decision if they haven't been given enough information?"[10] Ensuring that everyone involved understands the information guiding decisions, as well as the processes through which decisions are made, is a prerequisite for having trust in those decisions' outcomes.

That being said, there are times when an apparent commitment to transparency can be weaponized, when used by leaders in the know either to obfuscate a situation by releasing a torrent of data or to force a desired outcome by creating anxiety and even panic. This kind of action is far from true transparency, as it masks the motives of those on the inside, who purport to bring others into the decision-making process but in fact have already determined its outcome. Misusing openness in this way is corrosive to the trust necessary for working together toward solutions.

Directness. In addition to transparency, a commitment to direct, open communication is a necessary component of building and maintaining trust in difficult times. As Katherine Skinner told me of her collaborative work in Educopia's early days, "when things were hard, we didn't try to pretend to the other partners that those things weren't happening. We didn't bad-mouth. There was no point in doing that. But we did make sure that people knew what they needed to know, so that there wouldn't be kind of grapevine-ish junk happening in the background."[11] Eliminating the grapevine, or the back channel, requires ensuring that everyone has a firsthand view of what's happening and is able to communicate about it directly.

Direct communication, especially where conflict is involved, can be extremely difficult. It requires some courage to take up such conflicts directly, without resorting to passive-aggressiveness or back-channeling or stoking social media outrage. As Rebecca Kennison notes, we turn to those means of communication as a form of comfort at times when we need to be sure that we'll be heard by sympathetic ears.[12] Dean Spade similarly remarks that we often turn to gossip or social media when we're hurt and need someone to affirm our position.[13] But while these back-channeled exchanges may make you feel better in the short term, they can cause mistrust to metastasize—and, in fact, to become attached to you, as those around you become wary of how you might be talking about them behind their backs.

As Spade points out, "Giving direct feedback is hard.... [I]t is easier to project negative feelings and malicious behaviors onto the other person and gossip about it. This is likely to feel bad and damage relationships. When a lot of people in groups or scenes are doing this, it can make for broad conditions of distrust, anxiety, and betrayal."[14] Learning how to give that direct feedback in ways that can be heard, and in ways that can strengthen rather than damage relationships, is crucial to building the trust necessary for collective work.

Documentation. In the complex organizational environments we work in today, it's not enough to communicate openly about the organization's status and plans or points of disagreement. Our teams operate in a state of flux, with new members joining and existing members moving on to new opportunities. If key information or decisions are conveyed in meetings or other conversations but aren't documented in written form, they're all too likely to evaporate, leading to confusion, contradictions, and chronic reinvention of the wheel. Almost as bad: if that information *is* written down but isn't readily findable or accessible, it may as well not exist.

As François Lachance points out, "Record keeping is where good management serves good leadership."[15] To build a coherent, reliable organizational memory, thorough documentation needs to be created and maintained, including records of meetings and their outcomes, of processes and policies, and more. Of course, the passive voice in the preceding sentence hides a *lot* of labor: who has the time to create such documentation, much less maintain it? And of course documentation is only as good as the systems that organize it. Even so, as software developers can attest, the only thing worse than writing documentation is not having written it.

Producing and maintaining a clear, complete, coherent record of policies, processes, and decisions becomes increasingly important as collaborations grow, as teams become distributed, and as more and more team members work remotely. The software company GitLab, which describes its work environment as "all-remote,"[16] includes within its extensive guide to building and sustaining all-remote teams a detailed argument for what it refers to as "handbook-first documentation."[17] The creation of this handbook, which is intended to be a "single source of truth" for all team members, is itself a collective project, designed to ensure shared ownership of team processes and goals and shared commitment to the agreements that govern the team's work.

Accountability. Perhaps the most important element of building and sustaining trust is acknowledging and responding to the moments at which it has failed. By and large we (and by "we" here, I mean humans) are not good at this. We tend to overlook the ways in which we've breached the spoken and unspoken agreements we've made with one another, and as a result we generally believe that we are more trusted by others than we actually are. Surfacing the small failures of care, sincerity, reliability, and competence that lead to breaches of trust can be extremely painful. The deep root of trust, nonetheless, is open, forthright communication, based in an adherence to shared values and principles and backed by a willingness to acknowledge and account for errors. Trust, at its best, is an action rather than a state; it doesn't so much exist as it circulates, enabling better communication and growing as a result of that communication. Trust is a virtuous cycle, expanding as it is nourished.

Being a virtuous cycle, however, makes trust far easier to break than it is to build. This happens all too frequently in organizations that claim kinds of openness that they do not follow through on, organizations that point to and then ignore the recommendations of systems of shared governance. If you open up a process in order to make it transparent, for instance, and you invite investment in that process on the part of a team, but then ultimately disregard the team's input without a full and forthright explanation of the choice being made, you not only throw away the trust that could have been built in this process of team investment and communication but you also undermine the trust required to get a team to invest in such a process in the future.

And then there are the breaches of trust that are more serious, breaches that stem from violations of the shared values and principles on which your community is based or from failures of accountability in response to such violations. Too many institutions have experienced such breaches—sometimes, as at my own institution, stemming from horrifying cases of sexual assault and harassment that have been ignored or covered up to protect the institution. These cases not only give the lie to the administration's claims to working within the values that the institution's community espouses, but they also demonstrate the deepest failure to understand that the institution cannot be protected if the people that it comprises are not cared for first and foremost. When it emerges that the administration thinks of the institution before its people, by allowing egregious violations of community norms to continue without holding the perpetrators accountable, trust is broken in an all but irreparable way.

In such cases, the path forward likely requires a full and painful accounting of the failures that allowed the violations to go unaddressed. This path might draw heavily on principles of transformative justice or practices of truth and reconciliation. Until the wrong has been fully addressed, and until the circumstances and the structures that allowed the wrong to occur are transformed, the community cannot trust that it will not happen again. And without that trust, the community cannot survive.

Communities fail for lack of trust in no small part because distrust is contagious: when I see that you don't trust someone, I wonder whether I should trust them, and in fact I may begin to ask myself whether I should trust either of you. The repercussions of such questions shouldn't be underestimated; as Feltman notes, "[t]he disaster of distrust in the workplace is that the strategies people use to protect themselves inevitably get in the way of their ability to work with others."[18] Building trust, and often rebuilding it, must be the first priority of anyone working toward institutional transformation.

Questions for Reflection and Discussion

- Which decision-making processes in your position are most difficult and least understood? How might the people you work with be included in those processes so that they begin to develop trust in your reasoning? What would help you trust your team enough to open up those processes to their input?

- How have failures of documentation complicated trust-building in your institution? What forms of documentation might help develop trust, and how can you and your team work to create them?

- Where have you seen the effects of failures of accountability in your organization? How have those failures produced or reinforced a sense of distrust, and what might be required to rectify them?

CHAPTER 8

Values

We live and work in a world that is deeply invested in assessment. That world creates an insatiable need to know how we're doing both individually and at an institutional level, whether we're working adequately toward our goals and how our work compares both with our own expectations and with those around us. The question remains, however, of whether we're assessing the right things, for the right reasons, in the right way.

In the business realm, such assessment often takes place with reference to a set of KPIs, or key performance indicators, which provide the metrics that a company or a unit within it has decided are relevant in thinking about effectiveness and productivity. While we may not use the language of KPIs in higher education, we have similar metrics that we track and assess. In a university library, for instance, the indicators used to evaluate units and services might include the number of patrons served, number of books checked out, number of articles retrieved, number of searches of the card catalog, and number of unfulfilled requests. In a college or department, the indicators might include the number of course sections that fill, number of students per section, number of students on waiting lists, number of majors, percentage of students who graduate within five years, and so on. These metrics allow a unit to assess its performance and determine how well it's serving its purpose.

Say the word "assessment" to a group of faculty members, though, and you're likely to encounter at least one who has a profoundly allergic reaction to the concept, becoming itchy and irritable at the very idea of being asked to apply such metrics to their performance. Of course, we do it all the time: every year we go through the bean-counting exercise of the annual review, reporting on our publications, citations, presentations, course evaluations, and the like. But every year we suffer through this assessment in much the same way we suffer through the clouds of pollen that choke us in the spring.

For many of us, this allergic response derives from all those numbers; assessment is in many instances tied to quantification, a deployment of Taylorist strategies for defining and rationalizing something as immeasurable and interpersonal as teaching or learning or the development of new knowledge. Boiling such a complex cluster of human activity down to a set of metrics and indexes that are used to compare us to one another, and that are aggregated to compare our units and our institutions to one another, manages to steam away the non-numerical sense of purpose in our work. Why, one might reasonably ask in the larger context of what we're trying to accomplish, do these particular figures and measures matter?

Quantitative measures can sometimes help us set goals: if we want to expand the impact of a community-oriented project, for instance, figuring out how many people we've reached with that project and how many we'd like to reach in the coming year can create a framework for planning. Assessing our progress within that framework can tell us something about the effectiveness of our outreach methods, and, if we can drill down further into the data, we might be able to learn something about which outreach methods have been most effective with which subset of our community.

There are a lot of things, though, that we can't learn from standardized, quantitative metrics. We can't ascertain why members of the communities we want to work with are engaging with us. And we certainly can't understand why they *aren't*. We can't understand what the purpose of building engagement is nor whether we're serving that purpose or merely growing a number. We can't fully account for the quality of the good that we're doing based on metrics.

With such limitations, it's easy to understand why quantitative forms of assessment might generate allergic responses. Metrics run the risk of distracting us from asking about our less readily measurable goals, their significance, and how we're working toward them. In response to concerns such as these, numerous educators have turned their student assessment practices away from the quantitative, moving toward "ungrading" and other modes of engagement that support the parts of student learning that an emphasis on grades can undermine.[1] Ungrading demonstrates that it's possible for assessment practices to help us focus on our deepest goals and our progress toward them, if we take the time to develop the right practices for those purposes.

Developing these deeper assessment practices has to begin with a careful articulation of the values we bring to them, values that help us understand both the things we're assessing and what it means to support their growth. When Beth Bouloukos described her work to keep Amherst Press's goals oriented toward what was most important, she told me about the press's need to develop a different framework for assessing their success. "Instead of *this many* books," she explained, "we're thinking about how [our work] creates equity in a system that is terribly inequitable."[2] Supporting equity in publishing, or in learning, requires developing not just new counting mechanisms but new qualitative modes of assessment that are grounded in values.

My own first experience of the assessment allergy came during my stint as a faculty member at a small liberal arts college in southern California, where the administration and the faculty were preparing for a visit from our regional accrediting body. The vast majority of the institutions over which that body had authority were large public universities, which were radically different from our campus not just in size but in every related pedagogical assumption. As a result, the kinds of questions and instruments that emerged from the accreditors were in many ways antithetical to the structure of our curricula, our methods of teaching, and our campus interactions. Asked by our administration to think about how we might assess student learning, several influential senior faculty members dug their heels in, resulting in the faculty saying no: it was not the Way Things Were Done.

This turned out to be a serious strategic error. It's true, of course, that assessment *as we were being asked to implement it* wouldn't have been useful to us, and it may in fact have been harmful to the practices of teaching and learning that we valued. But the response from that accrediting agency to our allergic reaction was, effectively, "too bad." The college, which had perennially ranked in the top 10 small liberal arts colleges nationally, was threatened with having its accreditation withheld unless we complied—and complied in precisely the forms that we had been handed.

Insofar as this cautionary tale has a moral, it begins by sounding more fatalistic than I intend: resistance is futile. That doesn't mean that there's no way out, however. The trick is not to resist assessment, which in our case resulted only in having inappropriate methodologies forced upon us, but instead to get out in front of it and take control of its shape. If the faculty had taken the opportunity to detail the Way Things Were Done—and more importantly, why they were done that way and the significant outcomes resulting from them—we might have been able to build a form of assessment that mattered for our own purposes and then persuaded the accreditors that we were both taking their requests seriously and our own goals and values as an institution seriously.[3]

All of that, it should probably go without saying, is a lot of work: articulating our goals and the means for knowing whether we're meeting them takes time and requires some difficult thinking and negotiation among colleagues. As a result, it's easy to feel as though the assessment interferes with the actual ability to get the job done. But taking that time for reflection is a key part of the job, if we want to ensure we're following through on the commitments that our stated values create. It's not a coincidence, after all, that *values* and *evaluation* share an etymological root. Reflecting on the role that our values play in the goals we set and the ways we mark our progress toward them can help us refocus our work, and our assessment practices for that work, not on an abstracted set of KPIs but rather on the things that matter most to us.

This is true of the many different forms of assessment in which academics engage every day, including grading, peer review, and a host of personnel processes, from hiring to annual review to tenure and promotion. Our busyness can lead us to seek out easily identifiable metrics despite their misalignment with our deeper scholarly values. Worse, our belief that we know "excellence" when we see it can lead us to make judgments derived more from assumptions and affinities than from a real engagement with the work in front of us. By pausing to articulate how we know when our students are learning, or when a piece of scholarship is important or when the work a colleague is doing is making a significant intervention in a field, we define what it is that matters for us and how what matters can and should be observed. In so doing, we can create assessment practices that not only work to improve the objects of the assessment—the learning, the scholarship, the career path—but that also serve to build stronger relationships between those being assessed and those doing the assessing.

The first step—obvious, perhaps, but not easy—is to begin by articulating the values that we bring to the work we do. Part of the challenge in this process lies in the plurality of that "we." It's often easy to assume, especially when we're working in collective contexts, that our values are shared and that our terminology is too. This is particularly an issue for those who occupy positions of privilege, who have not been marginalized, as even well-meaning, progressive members of dominant groups frequently can fall into the trap of taking their values to be universal. Surfacing and discussing those values is a necessary part of the process of their articulation, and so is thinking deeply with the varied experiences and perspectives that all members of our institutions bring to their work.

The particularity of our experiences and perspectives lies at the heart of our values, which may be one of the reasons why dominant institutions often exclude those values from decision-making processes: values are thought to be subjective and personal, and we're supposed to be striving for objectivity and impartiality. But as Iris Marion Young reminds us, the entrance of "substantive personal values" into decision-making processes isn't a problem to be eliminated; rather, "the entrance of particular substantive values into decisions is inevitably and properly part of what decisionmaking is about."[4] In fact, as Frederic Laloux argues, "act[ing] from wholeness calls for more than rational decision-making alone"; it demands working with the self and its values and assumptions rather than trying to get them "out of the line of fire."[5] Excluding the personal and the subjective and the differences they're based in is itself a value. As the HuMetrics HSS team notes in the white paper "Walking the Talk," "[t]he danger is not simply that unexamined prejudice will inform our decision, but also that a naive understanding of objectivity will prevent us from recognizing the biases that condition all judgment."[6]

The HuMetrics HSS initiative, a collaboration working to develop "humane metrics" for conducting various kinds of assessment in the humanities and social sciences, initially came together around the problems created by that naive sense of objectivity. As the team notes, they began their project "by asking what on its surface seemed a simple question: What would it look like to start to measure what we value, rather than valuing only what we can readily measure?"[7] As they worked, however, that question opened up several thornier ones. The team could sketch out their sense of "scholarly values," but there were significant problems with doing so:

> Could we presume these values were universal? (We could not.) How might we craft a framework that allowed for adaptability if not universality? (Certainly not by drawing solely on the experiences of the core team.) Could statements of values serve as markers of aspiration, rather than traps that limit scholarly invention? (That is the plan.) What potential indicators and evaluation practices could exist if we started from a set of values, rather than starting simply from what we could measure? (If nothing else, practices that better represented the work in the humanities and social sciences.)[8]

As a result, the HuMetrics team spent several years conducting workshops and discussions, leading them to a values-oriented framework, which then formed the basis for an extensive interview-based research project.

For "Walking the Talk," the team conducted 123 interviews across the institutions making up the Big Ten Academic Alliance, speaking with administrators, faculty members, librarians, and other personnel involved in various aspects of tracking, measuring, and assessing impact and productivity in the context of promotion and tenure reviews. Their research indicated that "evaluation policies and the cultural practices that surround them are not only misaligned with work scholars find personally meaningful, they are also out of joint with the very values many institutions of higher education identify as core to their mission."[9] Even worse, their interviews uncovered a sense of futility around attempts to change these processes and policies: "Whether it is because of willful ignorance about how tenure and promotion processes are determined, unacknowledged investment in the idea that merit equates to success in a hierarchical system, a feeling of being overcome by the enormity of a decades-long problem, or a trepidation to poke an already irascible bear, it seems that no one feels that they have sufficient agency, authority, or energy to change the system, although there is broad recognition that the system is broken."[10]

Working through these anxieties and disavowals requires something more than any individual—even an individual vested with significant positional authority—can accomplish. The HuMetrics report makes a significant number of recommendations for steps that can begin to transform tenure and promotion processes for the better. Some of them, such as using offer letters or other hiring documents to align faculty assignments with both institutional values and faculty aspirations, require the participation of deans and other academic administrators. Others, including participating in values-based workshops at the unit level and revising unit-level governing documents, depend on collective action among the faculty, but those efforts have the potential to transform not merely a specific evaluative process but also an entire faculty culture.

In fact, articulating the values that we bring to our work has the potential to transform many of its assessment-related aspects. Grading, for instance: as I mentioned above, many instructors are exploring forms of contract-based grading, or ungrading, that free them—and more importantly, their students—to focus on the parts of the learning experience that matter most, rather than obsessing over the mathematics of rating and ranking. Similarly, peer review procedures that allow for open, honest discussion among colleagues might better allow us to support one another in advancing work across our fields than do the always tense and often competitive exercises in gatekeeping that we traditionally employ.[11]

A word of caution, however. The values that we articulate as the basis for such reimagined assessment cannot simply be named once and assumed thenceforward. Rather, these values require ongoing assessment and re-articulation, both to ensure that they're guiding our work how we want and to account for the ways that our thinking will necessarily continue to evolve. Trevor Owens, director of digital services at the Library of Congress, described to me the process through which his team considers, as part of their project close-out meetings, how their chosen values are instantiated in their work. If collaboration is a stated team value, for instance, they might reflect on the ways the project supported and encouraged collaboration and on how the next project might do so even better.[12]

It's not unlikely that the team, on reflection, might decide that the value, as they'd named it, doesn't fully get at what they want it to mean, and thus that the values statement itself requires revision. The process of articulating a collective set of values is of necessity a recursive one, which will likely never reach a finalized state. Still, connecting the naming and defining of values with the development of methods of evaluation is a necessary part of building an assessment system that supports those values rather than working at cross-purposes with them. This is especially true when the object of our assessment is people and not programs: ensuring that we're evaluating the right things requires us to think long and hard about what we value and why, and then to develop means of zeroing in on those things that we value.

Questions for Reflection and Discussion

- What are the highest values you hold for yourself and your work? How would you want to be assessed according to those values?

- What might a process of annual review based on the articulation of values, goals, and plans for reaching them look like?

- How are members of your team or your organization held accountable for upholding the values that the community has established? What processes are in place for upholding and reinforcing those values?

CHAPTER 9

Listening

So far, we've explored the problematic state of academic leadership, including its all-too-frequent confusion with management; we've considered the importance of centering leadership around people rather than institutions; and we've emphasized the crucial roles of trusting relationships and a focus on values in leading for transformative change. Ensuring that leadership doesn't warp into a top-down mode of aligning everyone with the vision of upper administration requires building a collective sense of purpose and allowing that purpose to evolve with the needs of the collective itself. It requires finding ways to support the members of the collective as they work toward their pursuit of that purpose. It requires that you know the people you're working with, understand their concerns, and learn from their ideas. Creating an environment like that requires—demands, in fact—that leaders do a lot less talking and a lot more listening.

This, suffice it to say, does not always come naturally. We live in a time and place where leaders, especially "thought leaders," are expected to have the answers and be ready to provide them at will. Edgar and Peter Schein ask of this moment how it is that we have "come to believe, now more than ever, that telling is the way to lead?"[1] Telling, in our competitive individualist culture, has certainly gotten mistaken for the way to win: we are surrounded by pundits and politicians (not to mention neighbors and even family members) whose primary form of persuasion consists of doubling down on their opinions by increasing their volume. The result, unsurprisingly, is increased resistance; those being told wind up tuning out, changing the channel, and digging in their heels on their own ideas. As Beth Bouloukos described it to me, her desire to transform scholarly publishing requires her "to be understanding and patient in order to open the conversation, because if you just go in very headstrong [believing] that your model is right and what other people are doing is wrong, you're not going to get anyone to listen to you."[2]

Telling rarely leads to winning hearts and minds, and it never leads to the kind of relationship building that leadership requires. It's for that reason, among others, that the Scheins argue that it's far more important for leaders to work on developing a mode that they refer to as humble inquiry, "the fine art of drawing someone out, of asking questions to which you do not already know the answer, of building a relationship based on curiosity and interest in another person."[3] By opening up space for others to offer ideas, to describe their thoughts and concerns, we create the possibility that we might learn something and that we might do something with that knowledge together.

Of course, that possibility can become actual only if we're genuinely listening to the responses. I explored the importance of listening as a practice of connection at length in *Generous Thinking*, so I won't rehash that here. The key, however, is recognizing that in every exchange, with every member of your broader community, you have more to learn than you may think. In fact, if you open yourself to it, you have more to learn than you do to teach.

Real listening requires being open to what you hear, rather than simply performing a listening state while other people speak. There's all too much of that taking place in our organizational lives: our planning processes, for instance, are filled with "listening sessions" where stakeholders are asked to make the time and effort to share their experiences and opinions. Our campuses are filled with advisory committees, task forces, working groups, all of whose members are asked to invest their energy and care in developing recommendations for the institution to act on. When those listening sessions and task force reports pass without appreciable results—with management instead making the choice everyone knew was foretold or, worse yet, with no result but a report that gets tucked away in a drawer—all that labor and investment winds up not just unproductive but counterproductive. It breeds distrust and disinvestment. Benjamin Lowenkron and Eric Elliott described the frustrations of having been asked to produce a proposal that then got shelved for two years waiting for an administrative green light. When I asked how things might be shaken loose in order to move forward, they noted that "simple communication could have solved a lot of this. Sitting us all down at a table for like 10 minutes and actually letting us do the talking and not them talking at us would have made a big difference."[4]

By contrast, conversations that result in substantive action— that invite further investment and involvement from those sharing their thoughts and that foster the sense that the institution is not just open to but is even acting on their contributions—can actively build community. Similarly, advisory groups that are truly heard by those they advise, and that are able likewise to communicate openly with the constituencies they represent, can build trust.

The factor that makes the difference in these two outcomes is a deep form of listening: not just hearing others out but genuinely attempting to understand, internalize, and act on what you're being told.

That, of course, is not to say that you can adopt or enact every idea you hear. Some ideas might be undesirable. Others might be desirable but prohibitively difficult. Those ideas still need to be spoken, and listened to, and acknowledged. If the forum is truly open, with broad enough participation, the difficult ideas raised from differing perspectives might begin to suggest possibilities. The goal in discussions like these, however, cannot be to arrive at consensus or to build acceptance for a plan that's already formed. Instead, these discussions might draw on the process of "political listening" described by Anna Lowenhaupt Tsing. Political listening, as exemplified by community organizers, serves not to resolve difference but rather to allow "difference to disturb too-easy resolution." Political listening works to get everything on the table. "To listen politically," notes Tsing, "is to detect the traces of not-yet-articulated common agendas."[5]

Political listening requires that leaders adopt an active but open role: not just nodding or taking notes as others speak but instead asking further questions that may draw out ideas and create connections. It's important to distinguish this kind of questioning from the "hey, I'm just asking" devil's advocacy that too often undermines the ideas being presented by suggesting that the listener knows more or better. In contrast, active listening requires genuine curiosity and openness. It also requires, as Arlie Hochschild demonstrates in *Strangers in Their Own Land*, checking in to see if you're taking the right things from what you're being told by recapitulating what you're hearing and asking whether you're understanding it correctly.[6] Political listening—deep listening in the service of building coalitions that can work together toward transformation—requires a willingness not to guide people in the directions we already want to go but instead to allow others to lead us.

In fact, the job of an academic leader, as Carolyn Dever described it to me, requires being "comfortable with being outside your area of expertise about 99 percent of the time. It's not only having curiosity about other people and interest in their work and other disciplines and so forth, you have to be willing to not be the expert."[7] If we're willing to do that—to put aside ego, expectations, presumptions, and instead dwell in and learn from what we're being told, what we might be missing—we can develop plans that will be better because they're more matched to the lived experience of those who might partner with us in achieving them.

Trevor Owens talked with me about his experiences in creating a new unit and developing its strategy, and he was candid about both the ways his leadership of this process worked and the ways it didn't:

> I think where there are spots where it didn't work as well, it was because I came in being like, this is the thing we need to do, and I need all of you guys to get in on it, and we're going to do it. Every once in a while that's the thing to do, just to get something going, but a lot of times when I would run into resistance, it was because I didn't understand the problems from other people's points of view well enough. It wasn't as good for that kind of relationship building, and the ideas would have been stronger if it had been more of a call to convene and figure things out together.[8]

That call to convene is among the most important tools of leadership: the ability to bring together a group of people and help them form a team, a cohort, a coalition, a community. Doing so requires a recognition that those individuals not only have a significant stake in the outcomes of a planning process but also have crucial knowledge about the problems that the plans are intended to ameliorate. Their expertise is often a part of the "big picture" that the upper administration is missing.

There are many areas of university life that suffer from decisions being made without adequate attention paid to this ground-level expertise. It's relatively easy to see this disconnect in student support services such as advising, counseling, housing, and so on: those who provide and use existing services know better than anyone what's working in them and what's not, but too often their concerns go unheard. This same disconnect is operative, as well, in areas like the curriculum. The curriculum at most institutions is owned and delivered by the faculty, and the expertise we bring to it is derived from a lifetime of immersion in it; who better to make choices about it? Our field-based expertise has led to a deep understanding of the forms of knowledge necessary to produce the student outcomes we seek.

What might happen, though, if we were to recognize that those outcomes *are not ours to create*? The outcomes in the end belong to our students. How might we develop means of listening to their interests in a way that would allow us to shape our sense of student outcomes in collaboration with them? A process of deep listening could provide the potential to work with students to build something entirely new, instead of reproducing our own structures of knowledge. We might discover, for instance, that many of our students have come to our campuses with different needs and intentions for their education than what we have assumed. Many of our students have goals that are far less individual than they are collective or social. Many have family and community needs and desires that their education can help to fulfill. What might be possible if, rather than finding ways to help these students conform to and succeed within the conventional structures of the university, we alternatively took our lead from them and their visions for the future? What if we genuinely listened to what they had to tell us, and learned from it, and built structures and curricula that centered their experiences and goals?

In moments of crisis and conflict, it's especially important that leaders listen carefully to those who have been harmed by the failures of existing systems and structures. It was the voices of the Sister Survivors at MSU, testifying about their experiences in open court and at great personal cost, that finally forced overdue attention to be paid not just to a horrific campus predator but also to the institutional structures that allowed him to assault hundreds of young women. Those assaults were enabled by many people who refused to listen when they were told what was happening, who refused to believe what they were being told, who refused to act once they'd heard. The case at MSU is far from unique: on campuses around the country, predatory behavior is not just ignored but is in fact facilitated by policies and processes that punish those who speak out against it. Genuinely transformative justice—justice seeking fundamental change in the circumstances and structures that enabled a harm—can only start with deep attention to those who have been harmed.

When you listen to the people most affected by your institution's policies and processes, you're likely to be confronted with a lot of things you'd rather not hear. They're painful, they're inconvenient, they're at odds with the ways you'd prefer to think of yourself, your institution, your commitments. But none of that makes the things you're hearing untrue. None of it is cause for refusing to listen. It is cause, rather, for some difficult work, both personal and structural, seeking ways to open yourself to the possibility that everything you're hearing is not only true but demands action too.

Questions for Reflection and Discussion

- What individuals or groups within your organization, or across the larger community, feel unheard? What issues do those community members face? How might their concerns and ideas be made the object of the organization's attention, shaping its future direction?

- What processes or structures within your organization would most benefit from community input? How can you make sure that input is heard and valued—and that those providing the input *know* that it is heard and valued?

- What kinds of input or feedback do you most resist hearing? Where does this resistance stem from? How do you experience it? How might you find ways to acknowledge your resistance while allowing yourself to genuinely consider what you're hearing?

CHAPTER 10

Transparency

If listening is one key component of the work of leading trans-formative change, there's a parallel requirement for the kinds of direct communication I encourage in the chapter on trust: shar-ing what you know as openly and plainly as you can. Healthy coa-litions require mutual understanding, and mutual understanding has to be built upon a shared knowledge base. Developing that shared knowledge base is an important responsibility of leaders seeking to create transformative change within an institution, beginning with transparency as a guiding principle.

Transparency, however, is a challenging idea, one that's prone to being tossed around without being adequately considered. In fact, Ari Weinzweig noted in the ZingTrain master class I attended that despite his commitment to open book management, he hates the term *transparency*, saying, "who wants to be see-through?" Fair enough! We might be better off using terms like *openness* and *honesty* when we're talking about people, after all, as these rep-resent the qualities of connection among individuals that create the possibility of trust. As applied to institutional processes and structures, however, *transparency* has value: allowing everyone to see and understand the workings behind decision-making, as well as the information that goes into and supports them, requires making institutional barriers see-through. Committing to transparency implies a commitment to opening up otherwise black-boxed operations to the examination, and ideally participation, of a broader range of members of the organization.

While I previously mentioned a possible misuse of something that might be called "transparency"—massive data dumps that mask the important signal with tons of noise and shift responsibility for difficult decisions onto a now-panicked community—the kind of transparency I'm pressing for here is one that creates responsible forms of inclusion in decision-making by creating a shared understanding of how organizational processes work, what information they take into consideration, and why the conclusions that result have been reached.

That is to say, transparency should not be used as a means by which leaders can abdicate their responsibility for making hard choices, nor should it be a mechanism for shifting that responsibility onto the shoulders of the collective. Transparency might ideally allow consensus to be built, but creating consensus is tricky. Dean Spade notes in *Mutual Aid* that consensus "encourages us to find out what each other's concerns are and try to create a path forward that addresses all the concerns as well as possible. It is based on the belief that people can cooperate and care about each other's well-being, rather than the myth that we are naturally competitive and greedy."[1] Working toward consensus may be necessary in intentional, non-hierarchical communities such as the political movements about which Spade writes. In some circumstances, though, requiring consensus can make it hard to move forward with decisions. Worse, in more conventionally hierarchical structures, the notion of consensus is easy to abuse. It sounds like a great thing, after all, for a positional leader to be able to claim that everyone is on board with their plan, but the creation of consensus within organizations without genuinely shared power often functions by squelching or ignoring dissent. As a result, in many organizations and institutions, consensus is at best a problematic goal, which must be approached with care.

Frederic Laloux, in *Reinventing Organizations*, explores the ways that non-hierarchical organizations—what he refers to as "Teal Organizations," which are structured to maintain shared power—have implemented decision-making processes that rely neither on top-down authority nor on the endless negotiations required in consensus-based approaches. Among these methods is what he refers to as the "advice process":

> We often think that decisions can be made in only two general ways: either through hierarchical authority (someone calls the shots; many people might be frustrated, but at least things get done) or through consensus (everyone gets a say, but it's often frustratingly slow and sometimes things get bogged down because no consensus can be reached). The advice process transcends this opposition beautifully: the agony of putting all decisions to consensus is avoided, and yet everybody with a stake has been given a voice; people have the freedom to seize opportunities and make decisions and yet must take into account other people's voices. The process is key to making self-management work on a large scale.[2]

In the advice process, decisions can be initiated anywhere in the organization. A self-managed worker who notes the need to make a choice about adopting a software package, for instance, is at liberty to make the decision but is required to seek advice from all who will be affected by it. That advice, once sought, need not necessarily be followed, but the decision-maker becomes responsible for the decision's outcome. This is a radical form of transparency: everyone knows that a decision is being made; everyone is able to ensure that their thoughts about it are heard; and once the decision is made, everyone knows who is accountable for its implementation and success.

Even where decision-making power is not so fully shared, however, transparency remains a key component of ensuring that there is trust in the process. When an organization operates transparently, everyone has access to the same evidence on which decisions are based, such that different interpretations of that evidence can be surfaced and considered. This doesn't necessarily mean that every single piece of information will be shared publicly. Some confidential information cannot be shared at all. Some sensitive information might be shared with a trusted representative body rather than with the organization as a whole. There are good reasons why some information might have this kind of restricted distribution—but transparency does require a careful consideration and communication of the reasons for such restriction.

If transparency functions by making the walls around otherwise hidden decision-making processes see-through, it creates a responsibility for leaders to give everyone insight into the ways that they go about making decisions. It asks leaders, having presented issues and evidence and other factors constraining decision-making to the collective for their input and discussion, to follow through by explaining the decisions that they've made, especially where those decisions contradict the input that's been given. This follow-through has the potential to create a greater sense of shared ownership over decisions, while being honest about the limitations of the process's openness. Without that kind of honesty, the glass walls that remain around the process can go unmarked—and unmarked glass walls are exceedingly dangerous, inviting people to run into them at speed.[3]

I've had the privilege over the last several years of working in a college whose dean, Chris Long, has made a commitment to transparency and who has acted on that commitment in a range of ways. One of the most transformative, I believe, has to do with budgeting. Budgets, perhaps needless to say, number among the most fraught aspects of any organization. This is perhaps especially true for universities and other highly complex nonprofits. On the one hand, there are rarely sufficient resources available to meet all of the institution's needs. On the other, the process of deciding who gets what is determined by forces that are designed to create conflict: allocations too often involve what feel like shady backroom deals, and even where they don't—where there's a clear formula that everyone knows about and adheres to—that formula can drive units into open competition for resources and for the majors and enrollments that determine their allocation. Such jostling so thoroughly undermines any kind of solidarity or even cooperation across units that one might reasonably wonder whether that's the goal.

Given these circumstances, the approach of open book management that I mentioned a few chapters back can be transformative for a business.[4] It could be similarly transformative in higher education. In fact, it might lead to the development of new values-oriented collective budgeting models, models that neither contribute to the calcification of the status quo nor turn university finances into a reenactment of the Hunger Games.[5] The kinds of transparency I'm advocating for here can help ameliorate the worst aspects of current budget models, but the real work of carving out a better path at the institutional level remains to be done.

My institution has not—or at least not yet—been subject to the worst of so-called "responsibility center management" budgeting processes; we've instead used an incremental model that doesn't rely quite so heavily on unit revenue production in determining allocations.[6] It's not a perfect model, by any means;

incremental budgeting tends to preserve existing inequities and can make it difficult to invest in new initiatives. In our case, new initiatives have been supported at the provost and dean levels through a small "tax" on all unit budgets, which provides a fund that the university or the college can distribute according to its priorities. The process for obtaining new allocations, however, is usually arcane: chairs make requests of the dean for new lines and other forms of strategic investment, and those requests disappear into a black box of sorts, with a result emerging that may or may not come with much in the way of explanation.

In spring 2019, Dean Long asked the college to approach the process differently. All the chairs of departments and directors of programs were asked to develop their priorities for college investment in accordance with a values-based rubric, making the case for the ways that their requests would help the unit, and in turn the college, better meet its collective goals. Those requests were then shared among all the chairs and directors, enabling everyone to see the needs that existed across the college as well as providing opportunities for units to collaborate with one another in thinking about how to meet those needs. The entire group then met to discuss the college's values and priorities and rated the requests based on them.

It was a messy process and at times an uncomfortable one, because many of us found it hard to rank the needs of our colleagues when all were so pressing. That discomfort, however, was at least partly the point, as the process asked all of us to understand viscerally the kinds of difficult choices that always have to be made in allocations such as these. In the end, the decision-making responsibility remained with Dean Long, but allowing those who lead the units of the college to participate in and advise on the process leading up to those decisions produced both a deeper recognition of the complexity of the choices that have to be made and a deeper trust in the reasoning behind them.

It was also crucial that this open process was implemented during a relatively good year, budget-wise, when there were strategic investments to be made. Spring 2020 was an entirely different thing, as COVID-19 led us into what gave every appearance of being a disastrous budget year. In response to a call from the upper administration to make significant budget cuts, Dean Long convened a cluster of task forces to advise him, in a manner similar to that of the year before, on ways to make the required cuts while maintaining the college's values. Those task forces, like most such groups in organizational life, were largely advisory rather than authoritative, and the knowledge that no one was going to be happy with the outcome made their work that much harder. There were moments at which several of us grumbled (and I admit to grumbling) that it would have been easier had the hard choices been made by those paid to do so. But including all the unit leaders in this deliberation allowed the college to avoid much of the suspicion and infighting that hard times too often produce.

The process worked to avoid such fragmentation in no small part because the dean continued to show up. Throughout summer 2020, chairs and directors had a weekly call—not an email, and not a webinar, but an open conversation—in which Dean Long shared with us what he knew, let us know what he didn't know, and did his best to answer the questions that were percolating up from our colleagues. His willingness to hear us, his acknowledgment of the difficulties we were all facing, and his determination to maintain an open dialogue, all were crucial to maintaining the trust that he'd built in better times.

There are limits to what such transparency can accomplish. It's unlikely that everyone will ever be happy with all of the decisions being made, no matter how open the process has been. Although a collaborative process such as our dean's did a lot to foster strong relationships among the unit leaders directly involved, it relied on those chairs and directors creating similarly open channels for communication within their units to stave off the inevitable conviction among faculty and staff that they were going to be hung out to dry. Anyone who has worked on a university campus will understand me when I say that there is zero chance of getting the entirety of the workforce on board with any administrator's initiative, but units within the college that had well-established cultures of open and transparent communication were able to weather the crisis and work together toward the best possible outcomes.

No decision-making process, no matter how egalitarian, will make everyone happy with every outcome, but the greater the transparency around such processes, the more everyone can develop a shared insight into the ways that decisions have been made. This shared insight can help everyone within an organization understand the higher-level goals and limitations that constrain or encourage choices, and it can build trust. Without transparency, none of that is possible.

Questions for Reflection and Discussion

- Which processes within your unit generate the greatest suspicion and complaint? How might those processes be made more transparent, such that the principles and data that guide them are better understood?
- What kinds of information within your area of influence might help avoid misunderstandings and ill will if they were more generally shared? How might you go about sharing them?

CHAPTER 11

Nimbleness

Organizational cultures are buzzing with claims of and calls for "agility" in the wake of rapid shifts in the political, economic, social, and environmental realms. This particular use of the term "agility" derives from the world of software startups, where "agile" is used to describe a set of project management practices that focus on short-range work sprints and frequent product updates. Agile, in this project management sense, is meant to be distinguished from long-standing software development practices described as "waterfall," in which a project is designed and built out in its entirety and released only once complete. Waterfall development is linear and structured: project specifications are fully elaborated before any code gets written, and a plan is established for the project's full production and implementation at its outset. Agile methodologies, by contrast, are iterative. Each sprint focuses on particular functions that are designed, developed, evaluated, and released in a cyclical fashion. The road map for the project as a whole thus remains flexible, and communication among developers, product owners, and end users is ongoing.

The two practices each have their benefits and drawbacks. Waterfall enables a team to keep a project's full scope clearly in view, but it can be inflexible and, in pushing release to the end of the process, makes user feedback hard to integrate. Agile obtains and responds to user feedback throughout the process, but as a

137

result, scoping and documenting a project and keeping focused on its long-term goals can be challenging.

Agile's adherents are legion, and devoted, and like many notions emerging from the tech industry, agile has transformed from a methodology into an ideology as a result.[1] As Trevor Owens told me in our interview, agile and its variants—Owens' team uses scrum—can help a team sort through a tangled mass of problems and carve off smaller issues that can be worked on right away, and this practice can produce insight into ways to solve bigger issues. But he also noted that scrum and other forms of agile run the risk of becoming ends rather than means, in which scrum becomes "the eternal answer" and, in particular, "the answer to why scrum isn't working is that you're not doing enough of it."[2]

This hints at something problematic in how the notion of agility has bubbled up in discussions of organizations and institutions as well: difficulties in effecting change are attributed to insufficient changeability. "The phrase that has been passed down to me from our C-suite," Benjamin Lowenkron told me, "is that a large ship is very hard to steer."[3] As a means of getting past the stickiness of the status quo, many organizations wind up prizing the ability to pivot over the actual results of pivoting. The ideological form of agility demands a disruptive flexibility that upends the ways things have been done, less so because they're not working, though that is admittedly often the case, and more so because they're not sufficiently "agile." This ideological ouroboros pops up often in the viral spread of Silicon Valley notions across the neoliberal economy. In higher education, the intrusion of "disruptive innovation," as Adrienne Kezar notes, has been particularly damaging: "Individuals who hold this perspective suggest that higher education needs to radically transform, discarding its traditional structure and culture. They perceive anything short of wholesale transformation as a sacrifice of the potential of disruptive technologies like online learning."[4]

Remember, for instance, the moment in 2012 when the board of visitors of the University of Virginia announced that then president Teresa Sullivan would be stepping down. The stated reasons for this ouster revolved around her apparent lack of agility: she wasn't moving quickly enough to "consider dramatic program cuts" in order to "keep U-Va. competitive in a volatile higher education marketplace."[5] The board's sense of the marketplace's volatility was in part driven by the appearance of MOOCs, or massive open online courses, and its conviction that "Virginia was falling behind competitors, like Harvard and Stanford," in the development of this "potentially transformative innovation."[6] Moreover, Sullivan was perceived to be unwilling to "shut down programs that couldn't sustain themselves financially, such as obscure academic departments in classics and German" in order to make way for transformative innovations.[7]

With hindsight, we know that MOOCs and other variants on online learning did not in fact transform the higher education "marketplace"—not because of a failure of agility but because MOOCs weren't cost effective and didn't produce good pedagogical results. (In fact, Udacity's founder, Sebastian Thrun, told an interviewer in 2013 that "we have a lousy product.")[8] We also know that the University of Virginia remains as "competitive" as ever, even with all those obscure academic departments. But this incident highlights the damage that the Silicon Valley–derived ethos of "move fast and break things" can do when corporate hubris overtakes any understanding of the values that focus on the public good.[9]

Moreover, it makes clear that the kinds of agility demanded by organizations and their boards today have little to do with institutional values and goals and everything to do with the market. As Charlie Warzel and Anne Helen Petersen note in *Out of Office*, the "defining characteristic of the flexible workspace has never really been freedom, no matter how it's been sold. It's always been worker precarity."[10] And in the production of worker precarity, the academy has been a cross-industry leader. Agility has long demanded that course sections be added or dropped from campus offerings at a moment's notice, so universities have moved to create a more agile—that is, contingent—workforce. According to the American Association of University Professors, fully 73 percent of the instructional labor on campuses across the nation was off the tenure track by 2016, with nearly 50 percent of instructional faculty in either part-time or graduate employee positions.[11]

Colleges and universities must of course be able to adapt to changing circumstances, but sustainable, ethical operations demand that they find ways to do so without creating unlivable conditions for the professionals whose labor they depend on—not least because, as is frequently noted but too rarely acted on, the working conditions of faculty and staff are, in effect, student-learning conditions. If our institutions of higher education are to embrace fully their responsibilities to their students, their leaders must begin to think far more creatively about their responsibilities to their employees and begin, as Bethany Nowviskie suggested on Twitter, to design and build "resilient *systems*" rather than relying on resilient *people*, which is "usually a sign that we let our systems fail."[12]

That creative thinking, however, cannot look like the dot-com version of agility. The academy must develop more adaptive ways of working, without question, but with a caveat expressed to me by Shannon Miller, dean of humanities and arts at San Jose State University: instead of embracing the "go hard and break things" mode of transformation, we must think about "the implications of that. What are the implications in terms of the human costs, and what kind of assumptions are there that elide the issues of the absence of diversity? So I don't mean go hard, break things, move fast. I mean, iterate, learn things, and appreciate what you learned along the way."[13]

If we approach adaptiveness not by changing direction every time the wind blows but instead by designing systems that enable us to read accurately and prepare for the terrain ahead, we might start suspecting that what is needed is less about *agility* than it is about *nimbleness*. I argue there's a difference between them. While I admit to never having climbed a single rock, my understanding of rock climbing is that it requires constantly reading the path of ascent, spotting not just the next handhold but the next three after that. We might oppose that studied progress to some Spider-man-like ability to jump from one place to the next without consequences, a form of agility that few of us will ever possess.

In case you think I'm making too much of a distinction between nimbleness and agility—and perhaps I am slicing things pretty finely here—I'm about to resort to dictionary definitions. Of course, the definitions for "nimble" and "agile" are connected. *Merriam-Webster*, for instance, defines "nimble" as "quick and light in motion: AGILE," and it defines "agile" as "marked by ready ability to move with quick easy grace."[14] The emphasis in both definitions on quickness and motion is, of course, what the contemporary business world is seeking, a "ready ability" to change directions just in case it should be desired.

Yet the *Oxford English Dictionary* adds something else to our thinking about nimbleness that's missing in contemporary agile ideology. The *OED*'s definitions of "agile" are, like *Merriam-Webster*'s, focused on quickness of motion, but the first definition of "nimble" presented there is "quick at grasping, comprehending, or learning; (hence) clever, wise."[15] This emphasis on learning and on wisdom is what's missing from most of the "move fast and break things" instantiations of agility: we need to be quick to understand the conditions ahead that might behoove us to move, rather than being ready to move for movement's sake. In this sense, nimbleness lets us draw on the knowledge we already possess even as the circumstances around us change. Might this resource not rescue us from agility's correlate, precarity, by allowing us to center ourselves and our communities in the values we have chosen to live by?

In practical terms, the distinction between agility and nimbleness might have a profound impact on university hiring practices. Rather than perpetuating the unethical habit of hiring underpaid part-time instructors to take up the slack in our schedules, we might instead use our planning processes to create positions for full-time, properly supported faculty with the nimbleness required to shift their teaching as needed. We might, in fact, begin to understand such nimbleness as a value in hiring, as well as in review processes, and reward it accordingly. We might even go so far as to develop more nimble institutional planning that could help reduce the need for nimbleness in individual employees.

Of course, developing such nimble practices would likely mean that we'd need to think differently about how we prepare graduate students for careers in and around the academy.[16] That work has of course already begun at many institutions, where degree programs now include not only training in pedagogy but also a widening range of skills that can ready graduate students for careers that can be deeply rewarding even if they don't look much like those of their advisors.

And what of their advisors? Not to put too fine a point on it, but too many senior faculty have taken the academic freedom that comes with tenure or its equivalent to mean "you can't tell me what to do"; they, or better yet *we*, given my membership among them, teach what we want to teach, which is often not equivalent to what our students need or want to study. The more successful we are in our research areas, the less likely we are to teach outside that narrow slice of our fields, leaving the more wide-ranging, introductory, or general-interest courses to our junior colleagues or to the part-timers we hire or to our graduate students. That is to say, we bear a share of the responsibility for the circumstances that have led to the university's deplorable hiring practices. All of us stand to benefit, though, if we reverse that gradual withdrawal into our specializations and commit to more nimble approaches to our course offerings across our fields.

This commitment may not only produce a form of solidarity among instructors at all levels, if everyone is available to pick up the slack, but also be a reminder of the reasons we joined the profession in the first place. In spring 2020 (just before everything went kerflooey), I was asked on short notice to pick up a section of our introduction to literary studies, a class designed to acquaint potential English majors and other interested students with close reading and critical analysis and a range of ways of talking and writing about literature. I selected a group of texts that had been published in the previous few years, all of which in different ways asked questions about who we are as we read and interpret the world around us. And the questions we asked again and again in class included "why do scholars read and write the way we do, and why does it matter?" It had been years since I'd stepped back to the first principles of the discipline, to think about why I'd gotten interested in the field and how I might engender a similar curiosity among my students. I was exceedingly nervous about how it would go, but it turned out to be the most joyful experience I'd had in the classroom in years.

Not incidentally, that joy was one reason among many that I found myself bereft when we had to move, with merely two hours' notice, to remote instruction for the rest of the semester. Fortunately, with but the vaguest sense of what was about to happen, my students and I had just spent what turned out to be our last session in the classroom discussing what we'd need to do if the unthinkable happened and we couldn't finish the semester in person. That glimmer of foresight and the conversation that followed didn't make the transition easy, but it did make it easier; we'd talked through some options for our work together online, and the students had started thinking about what they'd have to do to complete a semester off-campus.

All of which is to say, we can all benefit from becoming more nimble, from using our knowledge and experience to shift directions and think about what the communities we're working with need. Again, though, I am advocating being *nimble*, not *agile*. My proposal for creating more flexible faculty positions should not be taken as a further inroad into what Gary Hall has called the "Uberification of the university," turning us all into on-demand content disseminators within fully neoliberalized institutions.[17] And it is certainly not an argument for eliminating tenure in the United States or similar forms of job protection in higher education in other countries. Attacks on tenure throughout the United States today make self-evident the reasons why these protections are required: so that intellectual discovery and communication can proceed without infringement. Rather, my proposal for flexibility must go hand in hand with the strongest possible argument for why *everyone* working on *every* campus should have access to the most important benefits that tenure can provide:

job security, intellectual freedom, respect, and a living wage. That, though, requires those of us who currently have those benefits to loosen our exclusive grip on them, to recognize the extent to which our ability to say no has made the working conditions for those without that luxury increasingly untenable, and to develop the flexibility required to make the institution sufficiently nimble so that it no longer yields to the pull of agility.

Doing so might enable our institutions to create more full-time, stable positions, knowing that as conditions change, the folks occupying them will be able to adapt. This kind of nimbleness might also help us rethink the categories of employment on campus in a deep way. There are areas of administrative responsibility that would benefit from having members of the research and teaching faculty able to devote time to them during periods when their other duties demand less attention. And there are folks in positions considered "support staff" whose academic training has prepared them to teach and whose work lives might be enriched if they were permitted to. In his discussion of this drafted chapter, Martin Eve described this model of nimbleness as "solidity of employment, but flexibility of role."[18] This kind of nimbleness in job assignments does, however, depend on a two-part recognition: first, that all employees on campus are fundamental contributors to the academic mission of the institution, though in different ways; second, that none of those ways of contributing deserves respect and reward more than others. Our institutions can simultaneously become more nimble and more just in their hiring practices if (and, I believe, only if) they are willing to rethink the hierarchy of categories in employment, from the ground up, by ensuring that all jobs on campus are considered, with reason, to be "good" jobs: stable, not precarious; nimble, not agile.

Questions for Reflection and Discussion

- How might your campus reconsider the hierarchy that puts research faculty above teaching faculty? How might you similarly reconsider the hierarchy between faculty and staff?

- What structures—within human resources and within academic and administrative units—would need to change in order to allow for the creation of positions that value and reward nimbleness?

- What lessons from the shift in spring 2020 to remote instruction—its successes and its failures—should inform the ways we approach planning for future semesters? What lessons have we seemingly already forgotten?

CHAPTER 12

Narrative

During the spring 2022 semester, I taught a graduate seminar called Peculiar Genres of Academic Writing. The proposition behind this class was that scholars in a range of fields are called upon—but seldom taught how—to produce forms of writing other than the journal articles and monographs for which their seminar papers and dissertations train them. The most important and most overlooked genre may well be that of narrative. Scholars are often asked to tell the story of their work, whether in the statement that accompanies a tenure review portfolio or in the narrative that forms the heart of a grant proposal. These narratives at their most compelling focus not just on the *what* of the work—a recounting of the phases of a project or an enumeration of accomplishments as they appear on a CV—but on the *why* behind it. They explore the scholar's larger goals, how the scholar has been working or will work toward them, and most importantly their significance for the field, for the institution, for the larger society.

The need to tell these stories about the reasons for our work, both to our colleagues and administrators and to the world at large, and the importance of telling them well, points to the significance of narrative as a form of evidence that could be better marshaled in the service of institutional transformation. Finding humane, values-enacted ways of working in the academy asks us to shift our focus away from the metrics-reliant, outcome-oriented enumeration and assessment of our work's significance. That end serves, in all too many cases, to discipline us and our colleagues into conformity with ostensibly objective standards that in fact privilege certain kinds of professional focus. Such a disciplinary end could be fruitfully replaced with formative, individuated, supportive modes of exploring our values, our goals, and our plans for achieving them. But if we're going to implement new modes of formative assessment, we need to get better at telling textured stories about our work and others' work in ways that compel understanding and engagement. We also need to get better at reading those stories and gathering their significance.

Given the importance of personnel evaluations throughout the academy, this chapter suggests how narratives might be used in the reviews we conduct of one another's work. Developing our ability to tell cogent stories about the work done in and around our institutions, has, in fact, far-reaching potential.

I imagine that a subset of readers who are situated in empirically oriented fields or positions might be put off by the idea of using something as mushy as "stories" as the basis for what ought to be a value-neutral and evidence-based assessment of scholarly work. In fact, some of my colleagues in less-empirical fields may have similar concerns, accustomed as we all are to having in our heads some target figure for what constitutes "enough" work to ensure we make it through the next merit review or promotion opportunity. Without a measurable idea of the height of the hurdle, many of us are prone to anxiety about whether we can clear it.

Both the drive to be as specific as we can about requirements for raises, for tenure, and for promotion and the drive to tie those requirements to empirically demonstrable metrics originate with the desire to ensure that evaluation is as impartial and objective as it can be. Such impartiality has to be imposed, it seems, to prevent bias from interfering, whether that bias derives from race, gender, class, or other categories of structural oppression or from chauvinism among academic fields. It's an entirely laudable goal. The question is whether the means we've created for eliminating bias are working. We want well-defined processes and concrete metrics that protect us from a bad boss, a toxic department, or a malevolent administration. Yet many of us can attest that those problematic people and structures still proliferate in the academy and, furthermore, that the processes and metrics as currently defined sometimes provide the cover of "objectivity" for highly discriminatory outcomes and epistemic exclusions.[1]

So we keep trying to root out those discriminatory outcomes by making our criteria for assessment *more* objective and, in so doing, come increasingly to rely on numerical evidence, such as how many articles a scholar published, how many citations an article received, and how many students an advisor served. We've even developed quantitative means of assessing "quality," in which black-boxed formulas like "journal impact factor" rank things that ought to require qualitative and, of necessity, subjective judgment. The goal of all these attempts at objectivity is of course to remove such subjectivity and individual judgment from evaluation, when, as we heard earlier from Iris Marion Young, what we actually need is *more* subjectivity, *more* judgment, *more* politics. Our focus should be on opening up individual judgment, surfacing its biases, articulating its assumptions, and creating accountability for the values we bring to our work and the ways we do or don't live up to them.

To do that—that is, to create processes in our institutions that are political in Young's sense, in which we bring to bear our

judgment and engage everyone in collective decision-making[2]—
we need more than just numbers. We need the story behind the
numbers. Where numbers can direct our interest in ways that
might lead to speculation, narrative can explain, compel, open
up. Narrative can lead us to understand the significance of what's
happening and can help us communicate the importance of the
ways we work. Narrative can bring both its writers and its readers
into a deep consideration not just of what is happening but of
why it is happening and of what it means for us as individuals
and for our organizations as collectives.

Don't get me wrong: narrative isn't always a source of truth.
Goodness knows humans tell themselves and others all kind of
stories to rationalize poor decisions and bad behavior, and literature is filled with unreliable narrators who are not to be taken at
their word. All narrative requires interpretation, as any literature
professor knows, and that interpretive work—which involves subjective judgment—is properly part of the decision-making that
would derive from narrative review.

We already rely on narrative in crucial ways across academic
work, even in the most empirical, quantitatively oriented fields.
Articles reporting on research in the bench sciences, for instance,
are narratives of that work, exploring the presuppositions and
questions that led to the research, the method of conducting it,
its outcomes, and the questions that remain. Numbers might be
a key component of the evidence presented in these stories, but
it's the narrative that gives them meaning.

For this same reason, most personnel review processes do not
simply rely on the candidate's resume or CV, or on any similarly
abbreviated list of or measurement of their work done, but also
ask them to produce a narrative exploration of the goals behind
the work, the ways that it proceeded, the challenges the candidate

faced, and the future directions they are likely to take. The story ideally presses beyond a dry recounting of accomplishments to reveal a thought process at work. By centering the review process on that story, by foregrounding where the colleague under review is headed and why, the moment of review can turn into a conversation about goals and how they might be supported.

The same is true of the assessment of that work by those responsible for carrying it out. Whether the assessment takes place in the course of a project (in the form of peer review of a grant proposal or a manuscript) or in the course of a career (in promotion and tenure reviews), evaluators are charged not solely with rating the work but with relating something of the story of the work's potential or existing impact on its field, in order to help improve the project or a colleague's chances of achieving their goals.

Again, none of this is to say that narratives are in and of themselves more trustworthy than numbers. Stories can mislead, they can deflect, they can delude. A highly compelling story might present no evidence of that story's reality or of the teller's follow-through. The news has recently exposed incidents of eminent researchers whose data were demonstrated to be falsified; those researchers put their narrative skill to work in the service of fabulation.[3] So the evidence presented in the telling of a story still matters. Nevertheless, that evidence needs to be an integral part of a narrative that can be tested through interpretation, rather than being left to stand alone as an independent source of truth.

Too often, though, in our insatiable desire for objective data, we wind up privileging numerical assessments of a candidate or a career—x number of grant dollars raised, y number of dissertations overseen, an h-index of z—rather than understanding those figures as steps along the way toward a more significant goal. Turning those numbers into narrative—focusing on the *why* of the grants, the publications, and so forth—presents an enriched potential not only for the colleague being assessed but also for those doing the assessing: assessment can in this way become a form of constructive feedback, in which we help one another think through our purpose and shape the paths that lie before us.

Even more, telling the story of our work creates the potential for drawing larger audiences into that work and its significance. Writing a grant narrative, for instance, asks a specialist on the frontier of a subfield to tell the story of the work they intend to do in a way that compels the interest not just of other specialists but of those in adjacent areas as well. The ability to get others invested in our work, to help them understand why what we do matters, is key to ensuring their support for it.

Telling good stories of the work we do, and want to do, will support more success in grant applications, more success in project proposals, and a host of other scenarios in which we can help lead others to understanding our goals. This kind of storytelling is a skill that must be developed, though, for it is not generally one in which scholars receive professional training. More graduate programs should include training in narrative in the service of professional aims as part of their curricula, and more workshops should be offered on campus to help those who stand to gain from developing greater competence and confidence in their storytelling. A campus that offers such professional development might well benefit from having more of its community's work made accessible and engaging to outside audiences.

In fact, the skill set required to translate technical concepts into compelling stories is sufficiently important to the academy that numerous colleges and universities have invested in hiring science communicators to bring the work of the institution's researchers to public attention. Many of these communicators are employed in the university's marketing and communication offices, which might make some scholars leery, but these communicators are typically highly trained in both science and communication and are committed to developing a deeper public understanding of what science is, what our institutions do, what researchers and universities stand for, and what we collectively hope to achieve.[4]

Telling *that* story, in fact, as honestly as possible, may be precisely what's needed to undo the damage that's been done to higher education by the relentless quantification demanded by the culture of rankings and league tables fed by venues such as *U.S. News & World Report* and *Times Higher Education*, among many others. Quantification leads inevitably to competition, and competition to more quantification, thereby raising an arbitrary set of metrics to institutional priorities, displacing the less quantifiable values and goals that should focus a university's efforts. As Marshall Sahlins has noted, these systems of ranking become an end in themselves: "Competitive and invidious comparison is the ubiquitous condition of American academic existence. Everyone and everything is ranked, creating hierarchies everywhere. That the rankings are contestable and in flux only makes the competition more obsessive."[5] Narrative isn't a panacea for the damage done by rankings, but it can keep us attuned to our purpose and our impact. Whereas quantification may lead to the privileging of exclusivity, where our institutions brag about the number of student applicants they turn away, narrative urges us to look closely at the students we actually serve and the ways we serve them, detailing in human terms how higher education can change lives and transform communities.

Telling our stories to ourselves is, in this sense, just as important as telling them to funders or to assessment committees or to the world beyond campus. Numbers may be persuasive, but they persuade us toward the right ends when contextualized by a narrative that explains their significance and creates a sense of connection to the work at hand. And it's through those narratives—the ones we tell to those around us and the ones those around us tell us—that we have the opportunity to help one another reach our individual and collective goals.

Questions for Reflection and Discussion

- How can you tell the story of the work you and your colleagues do in ways that will draw others into the significance of that work?
- How might narrative be used to help establish the importance and priority of new directions that your unit or campus is considering?
- What can the story of your work convey that the usual form of the annual report cannot?
- What stories inside or around your institution need to be told? What support might make it more possible to tell them?

CHAPTER 13

Sustainability

A set of values loosely grouped under the rubric of "sustainability" has of late achieved prominence in institutional rhetoric. I say "loosely grouped" because sustainability may refer to several different ideas, all of which are grounded in a desire to create the conditions that will allow us to continue doing tomorrow what we're trying to do today.

Many of the conversations about sustainability in higher education focus on responding to climate change, as students and faculty press our colleges and universities to make as little negative impact—and as much positive impact—on the environment as possible. This is a crucial set of concerns for all of us to attend to, especially at the institutional level, where disinvestment in fossil fuels and reinvestment in green technologies and practices could have important effects. The Association for the Advancement of Sustainability in Higher Education has responded to the need for action in this area by creating the Sustainability Tracking, Assessment, and Rating System, or STARS, a framework designed to incentivize educational institutions to report their work to reduce their campus's carbon footprint.[1] All reporting institutions receive the Reporter designation, and those that meet certain points receive a rating, from bronze through platinum, which they can use to promote their institutional good works toward environmental sustainability.

In broader nonprofit circles, however, sustainability often has a somewhat different inflection. Sustainability for these organizations frequently hinges on the financial, that is, the organization's need to bring in sufficient revenue or philanthropic support to cover its expenses and continue its operations. Many nonprofits balance on a knife's edge, especially in hard economic times, and often must spend significant time and resources on fundraising or other income-generating activities, which have the potential to steal focus from the organization's primary reason for being. Sustainability in this context is double-edged: without the ability to generate revenue, the organization cannot continue doing its work; on the other hand, focusing on revenue generation can pull the organization away from its purpose.

Both of these senses of sustainability, and the difficulties that they present, are crucial for leaders in higher education to consider. Educating our students without doing everything we can to ensure that the planet we're leaving them will be habitable is an exercise in what Lauren Berlant called "cruel optimism."[2] Training our efforts on revenue generation to the detriment of the purposes our institutions are meant to serve is a component of the "great mistake" that Chris Newfield argues has undone higher education in the United States.[3] But there are aspects of sustainability that both connect and exceed the responsibilities we have to stewarding the planet and to securing our finances. For instance, Sayeed Choudhury described sustainability to me as "the transference of hope over periods of change."[4] That transference of hope can be assisted by our work toward environmental and fiscal sustainability, but it requires something more as well.

The something more might be called social sustainability. I choose the term "social" to point to the need for having a group of people who commit themselves—not just to their shared goal but to the members of the group. In other words, sustainability for collective projects requires the collective to dedicate themselves to the thing they're doing together as well as the very idea of being "together." This social aspect is, I increasingly believe, a necessary precondition for any other kind of sustainability that we're hoping to work toward. It's the "community" in community-supported software, the "shared" in shared infrastructure, and the "public" in the public good. It's the "mutual" in mutual aid.

An essential understanding of this relationship between sustainability and the public good derives from the work of Elinor Ostrom. Ostrom's long-term study of common-pool resource management led her to argue that the conventional wisdom underwriting the work of many economists—for one, that the "tragedy of the commons" was inevitable—was simply not so. In fact, she argued forcefully, community-based systems and structures for ensuring the sustainability of common-pool resources were indeed possible, provided that the right modes of self-organization and self-governance were in place.

Common-pool resources are one of four types of "goods" categorized by economists based on whether they are excludable, meaning that individuals can be prevented from using them, and whether they are rivalrous, meaning that one individual's use precludes another's. Public goods are those resources that are both nonexcludable and nonrivalrous, meaning not only that no one can be prevented from using them but also that they do not get "used up"; they remain available even as others use them. In this category—at least theoretically—we might include clean air and water as well as roads and other public services. Private goods, on the other hand, are both excludable and rivalrous; their use can be restricted to those who pay for them, and their consumption by one customer can reduce their availability for others. These private goods are most frequently market-based, often produced and sold for profit.

A third category is that of club goods, which are excludable but nonrivalrous; use of these goods is restricted to paying customers, but the goods themselves aren't depleted by any one customer's use. Here we might point to services like internet access (which of course raises a question about whether internet access *should* be a public rather than a club good). And, finally, there are common-pool resources: those goods that are nonexcludable but rivalrous. Because no one can be prevented from using them, but their use diminishes their availability, economists have assumed these resources are susceptible to what they have termed the tragedy of the commons, or the putatively inevitable overuse of shared natural resources.

At the root of the tragedy of the commons lies the "free-rider problem," which posits that when individuals cannot be prevented from using commonly held resources, nor be compelled to contribute to their management and upkeep, some number of individuals will avail themselves of the resources without contributing to their support. As the number of free riders grows, the resources become prone to overuse and eventually become unsustainable. This problem has traditionally led economists to conclude that preventing the tragedy of the commons depends on external regulation, whether through privatization or nationalization of the resources involved.

Elinor Ostrom's work focused on undoing that conclusion. In her 1990 book, *Governing the Commons: The Evolution of Institutions for Collective Action*, she points out that economic constructs such as the tragedy of the commons and the free-rider problem are based on a particularly pessimistic view of human possibility, one that mires analysis in its own metaphor. She writes,

What makes these models so dangerous—when they are used metaphorically as the foundation for policy—is that the constraints that are assumed to be fixed for the purpose of analysis are taken on faith as being fixed in empirical settings, unless external authorities change them. . . . As long as individuals are viewed as prisoners, policy prescriptions will address this metaphor. I would rather address the question of how to enhance the capabilities of those involved to change the constraining rules of the game to lead to outcomes other than remorseless tragedies.[5]

Ostrom's work thus explored ways of organizing collective action that could "enhance the capabilities of those involved" to ensure the sustainability of the commonly held resources on which they depend.

While Ostrom focused on natural resources such as fisheries, the problems she described, and the potential solutions she explored, present some important lessons for institutions of higher education. The first is, as I argued in *Generous Thinking*, that we've allowed higher education—and increasingly primary and secondary education as well—to be transformed from a public good into a club good. What should be a nonexcludable process of making knowledge available to the world has been gradually transformed, through tuition and subscriptions and other paywalls, into an excludable privilege. As with internet access, if you can afford the price of admission, then you get access to a wealth of opportunities, but if you can't . . . you don't.

Second, the case of higher education makes clear that public goods are often renewable but not infinitely so. Clean air will not stay clean without oversight. Fresh water is sold to corporations that interrupt its provision to the communities that rely on it. Roads have to be managed and re-paved. (Ask my colleagues in

Michigan about this one.) Public goods require a collective commitment to maintain them—and that commitment, not just to the goods but to the idea of the "public" itself, is part and parcel of social sustainability.

Ostrom's work demonstrates to us that with well-designed collective oversight we can avoid the tragedy of the commons, but that oversight requires a commitment to our togetherness. In fact, it requires rethinking the structure of our institutions in ways that manifest that commitment. If our colleges and universities were modeled not on the corporation but on the co-op, an organization in which every member has an owner's stake in its success and a voting voice in its governance, we might better ensure their sustainability without falling back on external regulation. While model cooperative institutions such Black Mountain College mostly seem lost to the past, the principles of shared governance that linger in present-day higher education call on all members of the institution to participate in its oversight.

What's more, this commitment should expand beyond the borders of the institution, to recognize not only the public as institutional stakeholders but also, crucially, the interdependence of institutions of higher education as a collective. Our institutions are too often pitted against one another, when the real threats to their sustainability come from outside the sector, from governmental and commercial entities that see colleges and universities as a source of private wealth rather than a public good. Higher education needs leaders who are capable of building and sustaining the solidarity required for all our institutions to succeed. Until our institutions are able to come together as a coalition and make a sufficiently compelling demand for the return to full public funding of higher education, and for the development of self-determined governance structures (rather than the externally elected or appointed boards of trustees and like bodies controlling our institutions today), we will never be able to achieve real sustainability in any form, whether financial, environmental, or social.

Finally, it's important to note that sustainability is itself insufficient. As Christina Katopodis has recently argued, "setting sustainability as the goal largely presumes we are, now, at a place of relative equilibrium and safety that only needs to be maintained."[6] We are, in truth, nowhere near such a point. Far, far more work—of the environmental, financial, and social sort—will be required to achieve a secure and just future for higher education.

Questions for Reflection and Discussion

- How might activities and groups on your campus that are focused on environmental sustainability become a field in which social sustainability might be cultivated?

- How might the practices of self-governance for projects, labs, departments, colleges, and other units on your campus be improved to ensure the commitment of their members to sustainability?

- What avenues can you imagine for restoring an understanding of higher education as a public good rather than a club good? What would be required for us to fight for such a just future?

CHAPTER 14

Solidarity

Right off the bat, I want to acknowledge that "solidarity" is a loaded term, in at least a couple of different ways. I've chosen it purposefully here, and I'll explore why in what's ahead. I hope you'll allow yourself to sit with what surfaces for you as you read.

In the introduction, I noted that crises, such as those faced in higher education in the wake of COVID-19, often occasion invocations of the idea of "shared sacrifice." At times this idea is invoked with a kind of generosity in mind: if we all take a small pay cut, we can help some of our colleagues avoid furloughs or layoffs. But the term "shared sacrifice" is often heard differently from how you might expect. Not only does sacrifice inevitably roll downhill, affecting most heavily those who are least well positioned, but the idea begins to suggest that *we* are in fact the sacrifice, offered on the altar of the institution and its financial reports.

The notion that our sacrifice is shared—that it is part of a collective determination to sustain the community we together form—depends on a deep understanding of what it means to be a community and on an equally deep faith, on the part of those asked to sacrifice on its behalf, that the community will in turn sustain them. It requires believing that those above are as committed to the notion of community as those below. And that belief is hard to come by, for good reason.

The concept of community is too often used to suppress dissent, to persuade those with concerns and grievances to put them aside in favor of a conflict-free norm. That norm, unsurprisingly, usually favors the interests of those in power, who benefit from maintaining the status quo. Moreover, where the community is encouraged to take action, it's often to fill gaps or meet needs for which institutions and governments refuse their responsibility. This is how we end up with school bake sales in lieu of proper education budgets.

In much of my prior writing on the future of higher education, I've leaned fairly heavily on the concept of community, whether in reference to the connections we build within our institutions or to the connections we create between our institutions and the publics that we serve. However, my growing recognition of the problems with what Miranda Joseph has dubbed the "romance" of community has led me to seek a more active term.[1] What I want from community—what I think many of us want— is a sense of belonging and a sense of shared commitment. I want to know that my community has my back, and I want those in my community to know that I have their backs as well.

It is that shared commitment that leads me to the notion of solidarity. Solidarity implies, to my way of thinking, not the blandishment that community risks falling into but an active relationship building and mutual support. Solidarity requires action.

It's crucial, however, to be clear about solidarity with whom, and for whom. As Mikki Kendall argues, white feminist calls to solidarity too often ask Black women, Indigenous women, and other women of color to put their concerns with racism aside in support of some ostensibly generalized sisterhood. "For women of color," she notes, "the expectation that we prioritize gender over race, that we treat the patriarchy as something that gives all men the same power, leaves many of us feeling isolated."[2] There can be no solidarity when the privileged insist that the marginalized set aside their own concerns to be part of "their" movement. Rather, solidarity requires us all to recognize that understanding the differing and complex concerns that others face is all of our responsibility.

Moreover, solidarity demands at times that those of us in more privileged positions put our own concerns and perspectives on hold: "as adults, as people who are doing hard work, you cannot expect your feelings to be the center of someone else's struggle. In fact, the most realistic approach to solidarity is one that assumes that sometimes it simply isn't your turn to be the focus of the conversation."[3] Sidelining one's own feelings isn't easy, but with a readiness to listen to and understand the struggles of others, and with a willingness to foreground the concerns of those around us, we have the potential to develop a real solidarity and to transform that solidarity into action.

One of my interviewees commented on the work involved in building solidarity, saying that "people fall into fantasies that the collective is something that forms organically and that we come together because people come together. There's nothing natural about it. There's a science and a technique to it." That technique is grounded in coalition politics, in which "it doesn't matter if I like you, it doesn't matter if we agree about [everything]." As long as we agree on a shared goal, we can work together toward it: "Think about activist projects that are about street safety, where you get people who are in wheelchairs, people with kids in strollers, people who want to be able to ride their bike down a little curb cut. We can all come together to make a material change that improves all of our lives in different ways."[4] Alliances like these can be short-lived. But larger changes in the institutions that structure our lives together require a long-term commitment, not just to our own goals but to one another's.

What does this mean in the context of the organizations and institutions I'm focused on in this book? First, it means returning to the claim I made early in this book—that people are the most important component of our institutions—and revising it slightly: *all* of the people that make up our institutions are its most important component, from the least powerful to the most. *All* of those people must be considered crucial to the institution's operation.

Second, we need to take a hard look at the ways that categories of employment are used to divide us, to pit our interests against one another. In institutions of higher education, discussions of these divisions often focus on the tensions between the tenured faculty and the not-yet-tenured, or on those between the tenure-track faculty and the fixed-term, or the full-time and the part-time. But we need to pay attention to the divisions and hierarchies within the staff as well, and between the faculty and the staff. And then there are the divisions between faculty and staff on the one hand and student employees on the other. All of us know that there are enormous differences in the benefits and privileges that these different categories of employment provide, and yet every position held by every employee is equally necessary to the functioning of the institution.

So how can we ensure that every employee, in every category of employment, is able to function as a full member of the institution? We must start working as if our institutions were genuine cooperatives, beginning with a notion of shared governance in which each member of the institution is a fully enfranchised participant in its operations. This means that all of the members of a department, regardless of position type, should have the right to participate in department, college, and university decisions. This suggestion will no doubt meet with a lot of resistance; in many departments, opening up the vote to non-tenure-track faculty, to post-docs, and to staff will leave the tenure-track faculty outnumbered. That points directly to the problem: there is a small, and in fact diminishing, number of highly secure employees who have the ability both to determine their own working conditions and to profoundly affect the working conditions for the rest—and who too often use that ability not to lift others up but instead to shore up what they see as eroding protections for their own roles.

I'll say it bluntly: defending the privileges of tenure worsens things for everyone else, and it winds up undermining the best of what tenure is supposed to be.

As I noted in the chapter on nimbleness, I am not arguing for doing away with tenure where it still exists—not at all. Rather, my argument is for looking closely at what we expect tenure or its equivalent to do and for extending its most important benefits to all categories of campus employment. Those benefits include, after a reasonable period of probation and evaluation, job security and intellectual freedom. Both of those benefits come with restrictions—there are ways to lose your job, even with tenure, and there are limits to academic freedom—but each is crucial to an institution of higher education's capacity to advance knowledge and to serve its publics without undue interference. And each should be considered crucial throughout the institution, not just for a privileged subset.

We need all members of the campus community to be able to reach their fullest potential so that the institution can thrive. Faculty members with active research agendas cannot achieve their goals without the work of teaching faculty who bear the weight of larger course loads, post-docs and graduate assistants who work in labs and support research efforts, and staff who ensure that the budgets and buildings function as needed. Faculty members who teach cannot do so without the work of their colleagues at every level, from the dean's office to information technology to housekeeping and dining services. Indeed all of us—and the "us" I'm talking to at this point is my most privileged colleagues, who like me have succeeded in a competitive system that promises to elevate us above the rest—need to recognize that the concerns of every group on campus are concerns that we should all share. We are deeply interdependent; creating a genuine collective on a campus requires that we be ready to step forward on one another's behalf, to ensure that all of our needs are met.

Solidarity, in other words.

Does solidarity necessarily mean establishing a labor union? Not always, though unionizing, without question, provides some key benefits for building cooperation and structuring the relationships between labor and management. Management often agrees: George Justice reports that in fact many deans prefer unionized campuses.[5] The process of collective bargaining can be challenging, and the resulting contracts can be complex, but still they are contracts, with legal standing, which clarify relationships and improve working conditions.

Of course, the existence of a union and the contract it negotiates isn't enough to provide genuine solidarity. That requires organizing both within and beyond the union itself. It may require cross-union connections as well. In my own institution, there are separate unions covering different employment categories, and during the COVID-19 budget crisis, the administration negotiated furloughs and salary changes with each union independently. Given that each has a separate contract, distinct negotiations are inevitable. But ensuring that the many unions on campus are in agreement with one another, and willing to defend one another, requires a kind of collectivity that operates at another level than the union.

At MSU, there came a moment in the negotiations when the faculty, both tenure-track and clinical, realized that everyone on campus was represented in this bargaining except us. The research faculty had resisted unionizing, like faculties at many other campuses around the United States, by insisting that we aren't *labor* but *professional*, and even mistaking the authority that we have on campus for management.[6] During these negotiations, however, it became clear that, as a friend of mine is fond of saying, if you're not at the table, you're the meal. The faculty were not engaged in a negotiation over the salary and benefit cuts we would take; we were *informed* about them. And worse: I heard through the grapevine that our inability to refuse those cuts was treated as though it were our acceptance and was used as a bargaining chip with the unions. The faculty, they were told, agreed to take this cut, so you have to give us something comparable.

In other words, the research faculty's refusal to organize, to understand ourselves as belonging to the collective of workers on campus, not only hurts our own ability to affect our working conditions, but it also undermines that same ability for those who *have* organized and are trying to work together. If we are to transform our campuses, if we are to create better working conditions for everyone on campus, we must *all* be in it together. We have to ensure that the secure, the empowered, the privileged are fighting on behalf of everyone else, rather than interfering with their ability to fight for themselves.

So I'm ending this call to solidarity by taking a strong "one campus, one faculty, one union" stance. We are all workers in the same enterprise, albeit with different responsibilities, and ensuring that we are all mutually supportive requires us to refuse being divided into categories and appointment types. Shifting to this kind of collectivist thinking is no easy matter, to be sure, especially not for those of us who have long been conditioned to believe that we operate willingly in a functioning meritocracy, that our achievements are individual and so our rewards should be too, and that we're better off when we can negotiate special deals—a course release here, an augmented budget there—by and for ourselves. As noted by my anonymous interviewee quoted above, cooperation does not happen effortlessly, as we often disagree with one another about a host of issues. Building habits of collectivity *in spite of these disagreements* will not only help us create a more equitable, caring community within our institutions, but it will press us to focus the institution's efforts on its broader social responsibilities, responsibilities that may best be served by functioning as a cooperative.

Developing a strong sense of solidarity is no simple matter in institutions and cultures that thrive on competitive individualism, but leading the way toward a better world requires that we start thinking about one another's needs and perspectives with the same urgency that we consider our own. As the authors of *Secrets of a Successful Organizer* remark, "Solutions are collective, not individual."[7] And as George Justice urged me, when I asked him what he thought it would take for us to build institutions that are more just, more equitable, and more generous, "take a look at those three terms—just, equitable, and generous. They are not separate there. They really need to come together, and it's going to be impossible in the future to have generous leadership in institutions that are not more just and more equitable."[8] Working toward a future in which our institutions of higher education are just, equitable, and generous means that all of us must take part in that collective solution.

Questions for Reflection and Discussion

- What are the effects in your institution or organization of the divides created among various position types? How do the terms of your employment place you at odds with one another?
- What kinds of concerns have your colleagues in other kinds of positions expressed about their working conditions? How can you use your position to help support those colleagues and their needs?
- How might you and your colleagues organize to ensure that you're all working together?

PART III
The Stories

In the course of the interviews that I conducted for this project, I heard some remarkable stories of institutional transformation and the leadership that helped bring it about. I've selected five of those to share here, including one story about a deep and ongoing struggle against the odds. These stories highlight the ways that the tools I explore in part II might be put to work in developing new kinds of leadership for institutional transformation. I've done my best to capture the significance of the storytellers' work, as well as the aspects of their voices that make the stories compelling.

CHAPTER 15

Transforming
Institutional Structure

GREG EOW

When Greg Eow became the associate director for collections at the MIT Libraries in June 2015, the library had long been a leader in thinking about the future of scholarly communications. The scholarly communications program in the libraries was created in 2006 and in 2009 began the work of implementing the MIT Faculty Open Access Policy. Chris Bourg had become the director of the libraries earlier in 2015, bringing with her a commitment to openness and to the transformations that had begun in digital publishing.[1] Eow's role, as described in the announcement of his hire, emphasized his leadership skills—including his "passion, intelligence, creativity, and commitment to diversity, inclusion, and transparency"—and noted that he'd be bringing those skills to the work of the "innovative and entrepreneurial" collections team, but it's not clear that anyone had a sense of the massive changes that lay ahead.[2]

As Eow told the story, when he first joined the libraries' leadership team, his portfolio of involvement included collections (which mostly entailed the purchasing of new resources), archives and special collections, and technical services (which included cataloging and metadata). Scholarly communications—the team, led by Ellen Finnie, which was implementing the open access policy, working to build the institutional repository, and managing a wide range of relationships around licenses and publishers—was not part of Eow's portfolio. Eow's initial idea to bring collections and scholarly communications together derived from his sense of the libraries' mission: "trying to create a nice, healthy scholarly communications ecosystem, not just being a purchasing agent but shaping the whole content and creation space."[3] So he suggested that the libraries create a department that came to be called Scholarly Communications and Collection Strategy and—rather astonishingly—that they move the entire collections budget and team into that new department, ensuring that its focus would be part of an overall vision for the future of scholarly communications.

It was an audacious plan, one that drew significant attention from the world of academic libraries when it was announced, but the thing that made it work was not the brilliance of the vision but the collective process of its development. As Eow told me,

> I didn't just say, here's my plan, what do you all think. . . .
> I started talking with my peers. I talked with Chris Bourg, and I was like, "Chris, what do you think about this idea?" And she's like, "I kind of like it." And then she hammered it out a bit, and we talked to this person and talked to that person. . . . I talked to my peers, and Tracy Gabridge, who's now the deputy director. "What do you think about this?" And then she would say, "oh, Ellen's a really good leader," and she would ideate with me. And then I talked with another peer, and they said, "well, this is what the title should be." In every conversation, the idea got more refined. It also got socialized, so other people started talking about it. I wasn't surprising people with it. Then I talked to Ellen about it, and Ellen and I started sketching things out and

getting excited about it and playing around with—well, what would they do, what would the workflows be, what would the title be, what would my title be?

The openness of this set of conversations, and the fact that each conversation was allowed to influence and shape the idea as it moved forward, built people's investment in moving the plan forward.

After he and Ellen Finnie had worked through the idea enough that they were comfortable with it, Eow started talking to the folks who would be most affected by it, the people who would be reporting up through a structure that, under the new model, made collections a subgroup of scholarly communications: "I remember I was a little bit nervous. Like, is there going to be pushback? This is going too smoothly. And I remember one librarian who was a really, really strong critical thinker—if someone was going to be a naysayer, this person was going to do it, and be really good at it, because [she's] really smart. And I explained the idea to her, and she went [pauses, nods slowly], 'Yeah, let's do it.'" All of these conversations, with everyone who had a stake in the change, resulted not only in a plan that improved over time but also in one that everyone was able to get on board with before it was implemented. As Eow noted, the process both refined and, importantly, socialized the idea; there were no secrets or surprises sprung on the team; instead everyone had the opportunity to provide feedback in advance and to see evidence that their advice had been heard.

This transformation coalesced a focus on the deepest values of the library, a recognition that the institution's structure must be organized in service to its mission rather than being an end in itself, along with a commitment to building a coalition that would support the transformation and work toward its success. The most amazing part of this story, however, may be its efficiency. Eow described the conversations he had—"lots and lots of conversations"—as "time-bound," working to move the idea forward in a focused fashion. As a result, "we went from the idea to launching this department, probably within a month."

Not all coalition-building processes will be that speedy, of course. But it is possible for a series of one-on-one conversations, conversations allowed to shape the idea under exploration, to result in a plan that faces far less resistance upon its execution.

Two things are worth noting here. First, both Ellen Finnie and Greg Eow have moved on from MIT Libraries into leadership roles at other library organizations. As Rebecca Kennison explains, "In both cases, what they learned about coalition building during the MIT reorg is now core to their success in their [comparatively] new roles, which are multi-institutional organizations in which all members have equal voice."[4] Second, the consolidation of the collections budget under scholarly communications is both revolutionary for what it says about the shifting relationship between the two entities in libraries of the future, as well as for the more basic notion that one unit might be willing to share control of its budget with another unit in service to a shared good. It's of course important to note that this happened in a relatively cash-rich environment; in most cases, budgetary consolidation takes place under austerity-driven conditions, which makes the work involved in developing a viable coalition more difficult. Achieving this level of cooperation is, if anything, even more important when resources are scarce—not in order to "do more with less" but to avoid territoriality and infighting and to create the conditions for collectively demanding more.

CHAPTER 16

Transforming Community

ERIC ELLIOTT AND BENJAMIN LOWENKRON

I grew up in Baton Rouge, Louisiana, the home of the institution where Eric Elliott and Benjamin Lowenkron work. I went to college in town, at Louisiana State University, and stuck around long enough to get an MFA in creative writing to boot. When I finally moved away, in 1991, the local options for postsecondary education were as they had been for decades; there were Louisiana State and Southern Universities, and then there was a smattering of vocational and technical schools supporting the trades. There was nothing in the space that community colleges fill today: low-cost public institutions providing access to associates degrees that might be an end in themselves or might provide a point of entry and transferable credit toward a bachelors.

Baton Rouge Community College thus filled a gaping need when it opened its doors in fall 1998, so much so that the institution enrolled more than 2.5 times the number of students predicted in that first semester: rather than the 700 students expected, over 1,850 entered. The campus has continued to grow at a shocking rate: in 2022–23, BRCC enrolled over 9,000 students; in fall 2023, that number jumped to more than 11,000, including nearly 2,700 dual-enrollment students, who have been strongly encouraged by the school district to obtain college credit while completing their high-school diplomas.

Meanwhile, BRCC employed 149 full-time and 179 part-time faculty in fall 2022. By way of comparison, LSU enrolled over 31,000 undergraduates in fall 2022, and they were instructed by nearly 1,500 full-time faculty and another 200 part-time faculty. Southern University, a historically Black (and chronically under-funded) university enrolled just over 8,200 undergraduates in fall 2022 and claims a student-faculty ratio of 18:1, which would suggest a total instructional faculty of around 450. BRCC's student-faculty ratio in fall 2022 was 26:1, and the "full time" workload for a faculty member is defined as no fewer than 30 credit hours per year for a 9-month faculty member and no fewer than 40 credit hours for a 12-month faculty member.[1] Serving the needs of a highly diverse student population poses challenges for the BRCC faculty, who do not have access to tenure or the support of a union; they work in an at-will state, on year-to-year contracts that can be terminated for any reason.

Benjamin Lowenkron and Eric Elliott have each taught at BRCC for more than a dozen years, supporting students in English 101 and other foundational courses as they work to address the ways in which students' primary and secondary educations have failed them. BRCC is a predominantly Black institution (PBI), and as Lowenkron told me, calling these students "under-served" is "too generous"—"these are *excluded* groups, these students we have."[2] In 2016, BRCC received a Title III formula grant from the US Department of Education designated for PBI schools; these grants are intended "to strengthen eligible institutions to plan, develop, undertake and implement programs to enhance the institution's capacity to serve more low- and middle-income Black American students; to expand higher education opportunities for eligible students by encouraging college preparation and student persistence in secondary school and postsecondary education; and to strengthen the financial ability of the institution to serve the academic needs of these students."[3]

Since 2016, this grant and its successor have brought more than $8,000,000 to the BRCC campus, enabling it to establish the Center for Undergraduate Student Achievement (CUSA), a locus for curricular innovation and student support. During the COVID-19 pandemic, when the campus's first five-year grant period was complete, the Department of Education waived the waiting period between grants and renewed its support for a second five-year period, enabling the work being done by CUSA to continue.

Things had gone less than ideally on campus, however. Between the inception of the first grant and fall 2023, CUSA had seven different directors, making continuity in program building all but impossible. The pressures on faculty and staff during the pandemic additionally led to significant burnout, and churn in the upper administrative ranks made things even more difficult—particularly in an institution whose "C-suite" is "so far away" that they can't pay attention to what's happening on the ground and yet "are so interested in controlling what's going on" that nothing can move forward without an official green light.

The effects of COVID-19 on students were if anything even more pronounced. Elliott noted that "prior to the pandemic, our average student age was probably 10 to 15 years older than it is now. Once the pandemic happened and students were forced to go online, students that were over the age of 30 just bailed because they did not have the acumen, they did not have the tech knowledge that younger students had. That was cross-ethnic, that was cross-class." The problem wasn't just acumen, however; the students also experienced huge gaps in technical access. They were far too likely not to have their own laptops or to have access to reliable internet connections.

Lowenkron described focus groups that CUSA conducted with students upon returning from the pandemic to find out more about their experiences; these conversations revealed that while their students "were mostly able to hold the line in terms of GPA when it came to their humanities courses, they tanked when it came to STEM [science, technology, engineering, and mathematics]. One of the reasons we found out was because of technology access." BRCC was able to provide some loaner Chromebooks, but those devices often struggled with the specialized software that STEM courses required, and students' financial aid packages often arrived too late to support the purchase of equipment and licenses. And more: the focus groups showed that students felt no sense of belonging on campus; they felt deeply "estranged from the institution."

As a result, BRCC used part of the CUSA funding to reinvent its existing student support center by opening the Digital Learning and Academic Support Center (DLASC) as one among a number of technology-enabled "Spaces of Belonging" being built across BRCC's campuses. These are spaces where students not only can find the equipment and network connections they lack and the technical support they need but can also find the community they desire. The DLASC provides group study spaces, noise-controlled study pods, classrooms for hands-on workshops, and more. Additionally, BRCC added a new type of tutor to its support offerings, hiring digital literacy technicians who could train students, faculty, and staff alike on hardware and software.

Lowenkron, BRCC's interim program director for teaching and learning technology, is meant to be one of three full-time administrators leading the DLASC, but between his appointment in October 2022 and the time the center opened in January 2023, the other two leaders involved, an academic tutoring director and a center director, had left for other opportunities. At the time of our October 2023 interview, Lowenkron had been running the center by himself for the duration; listings for the other positions had twice been opened and closed by the central administration with no apparent movement on hiring. Lowenkron nevertheless had put together a team of 20 peer tutors, and the center saw over 5,000 clients in the 10 months since its opening. As he told me, "This is very much a system that relies upon those with broad shoulders to carry a lot of the weight."[4]

Elliott applied for one of the DLASC administrative positions when it was first listed but opted not to reapply when it was re-opened, deciding instead to focus on the ways he could support students in the classroom. During the pandemic, as one of the faculty champions working within CUSA, he was asked to put together a workshop for an interdisciplinary group of both faculty and students to be conducted via Zoom. This workshop drew on his work in the Introduction to World Mythology course he'd taught for some time, which focuses on the archetypal structure of the hero's journey. This structure enabled faculty and students to talk about how the pandemic was affecting their work on campus and to think about their progress and the support they needed to achieve their goals. Such a workshop, Elliott said, is especially important for helping faculty recognize that their students "are coming to college without the ancestral readiness that a lot of us take for granted" and for helping the students track their own journeys and the allies that can help them along the way.

The workshop was highly successful, drawing praise from faculty participants in both humanities and STEM fields, and the most recent director of CUSA asked Elliott to put together a curriculum plan for a cohort program that would include workshops, events, and more. That proposal has been waiting for a green light for nearly two years. When asked what's needed to get that green light, Lowenkron noted that it's mostly a matter of "convincing people to tell us to do what we suggested we'd do." He likened it to "the old classroom trick" of bringing the conversation around such that the desired ends emerge naturally. "I am at heart an evolutionary," he said, "not a revolutionary."

In the meantime, Elliott has continued doing what he called "covert stuff" toward creating change in the classroom, while Lowenkron has worked on bringing change through his administrative role. "[W]here I can effect [change] here is through our peer tutors," explained Lowenkron. "They know, because I tell them explicitly, I'm trying to create autonomous leaders." This grassroots, student-centered work, coupled with the tightness of the relationship the two have together—they are 18 years into what Elliott described as "brother-from-another-mother-hood"—allows Elliott and Lowenkron to sustain each other and to maintain the energy required to work toward institutional change.

And their students, as both of them emphasized, are allies in this work. As Elliott put it, "the connections that I've been lucky enough to make with students have radically transformed my life, and I think radically changed the way that I would view this job were it not for those students. I'd be gone, doing who knows what." Both Elliott and Lowenkron were brought into the grant project based on student recommendations, and each has worked tirelessly to help students succeed. They are committed to this work because, in Lowenkron's words, "If you are an open enrollment institution, then that means you have to be *open enrollment*. That means any student that comes through, you're saying, 'you can learn, you can grow. And we are here to serve you." That means you cannot put up these barriers and say, 'well, you're not ready for this or that.'" By focusing on the students, by centering their needs and being willing to get creative (and even covert) with their methods, Elliott and Lowenkron have been able to help students "become in charge of their own destinies [so that] they get to tell us what their success looks like, not the other way around."

CHAPTER 17

Transforming Hiring

ROBIN SCHULZE

I was first encouraged to talk with Robin Schulze, dean of the College of Arts and Sciences at the University at Buffalo, by Evviva Weinraub Lajoie, vice provost for UB's University Libraries. "She's looking at different ways of approaching hiring and thinking about how to bring different voices into the hiring process," she told me.[1] Hiring is of course one of the ways that we try to create change on campus, but there hasn't been much transformation of the hiring process itself in recent years. Hiring is subject to many campus-level policies that aim to keep the process fair, but whether the outcomes it produces are indeed fair—or even capable of creating the deep cultural change on campus that we need today—remains an open question. As a result, I was excited to hear about a new approach.

Schulze came to her role at UB from the University of Delaware, where she served as the associate dean for the humanities, and prior to that from Penn State University, where she was the chair of the Department of English. One of her key goals as dean was to build a more racially diverse and equitable faculty, one that could better support the university's increasingly diverse student population. This change was a top-level university priority, she told me, both because prospective students are increasingly deciding where to enroll according to the representation they see on campus and because UB was at the bottom of the rankings for faculty diversity published by the Association of American Universities. But transforming the racial and ethnic makeup of the faculty would require more than the usual attention to good hiring practices; an entirely new approach, with a new mindset, was in order.

Schulze had two key things working in her favor. She had previously worked with Teri Miller, the late senior vice chancellor for strategic initiatives and chief diversity officer for the system of the State University of New York, on a grant designed to establish the Center for Diversity Innovation at UB. As a result, Schulze had a track record of success and the attention of her provost and president. And, crucially, she had what she called "the secret sauce of SUNY," which is a State of New York policy permitting targeted hiring: "If we're underrepresented in a particular category of individual, I can go out and say, 'there's a job for you here if you want it,' rather than ask you to apply for an open search."[2]

The thing that Schulze believes made this transformative program work didn't come from above, however—not from the state and not from the upper administration. It succeeded thanks to her recognition that however hierarchical UB might appear from the outside, it is in fact quite a bottom-up culture. As a result, she "rounded up the entire college, and had every department in the college identify individuals that they would want to approach." The next step drew on a radical form of transparency:

> Rather than just leave it at that, we took it [to the college], so that every department shared with every other department all the individuals they wanted to approach. We had a discussion of how they could all work together, what we were going to do

to support them, how they would create new intellectual areas or build on things we were already good at. Then we had the departments report to each other, and actually rank their candidates. That was done sector by sector inside the college—so the arts and humanities did it, then social sciences did it, then natural sciences and math. And then we came together as an entire college . . . so that everybody saw every other individual that every department wanted to recruit. We came up with a ranked list out of the entire college. And that, to my understanding, was the first time that the college had ever come together as an entire college to think about things that could go on across all disciplines, across all departments, and think about what we were going to all build together. On the basis of that, we took a giant report up to my provost that had 125 names on it.

That report asked for a *lot* of money, Schulze said, but it was backed by her confidence that the college, working together, could pull off this transformation. And the provost came through with "one of the biggest investments the university had ever made," allowing the college to go forward with an initial recruitment of 33 new hires.

Schulze managed the recruitment efforts herself because she wanted to communicate to all of the candidates that this was a college-level initiative, that "we know we need to change things, and here are all the things we're going to be doing." At the time she and I talked, the college had successfully hired 15 new faculty members and was still actively recruiting another 8. Given the complexities presented by COVID-19 and other personal factors, several candidates immediately said that they couldn't consider the offer, but Schulze left the door open by saying, "that's fine for now, but if things ever change for you, give me a call." That openness led to one additional hire.

Asked what factors made this initiative successful, Schulze identified the importance of UB's bottom-up orientation and the process of getting every member of the college faculty to understand that "if we're going to participate in this, certain things have to change. They have to change culturally. They have to change policy-wise. They have to radiate up from the bottom, and then we have to have everybody in alignment before we do this." That approach is particularly important in the academy. Schulze pointed out the number of universities that she's seen pour money into initiatives, conceived and pushed down from above, that did not avail the desired results. The success of her approach within her college led the upper administration to ask her to report to the other colleges of UB on how it was done, and at least one has since created a similar bottom-up initiative leading to nine hires.

The work of the initiative is not done, Schulze added, and what lies ahead will require even more transparent communication: "The onus on us is to retain all these individuals. So that's what we're working on now. What are our major retention plans we're going to put together? How are we going to round up the resources to do that? . . . And that again is not something that I'm making up. It's something that we're asking these persons directly. You know, anything that you kind of imagine without actually directly consulting the constituency is probably not going to work." Focusing on retention at the outset is a crucial shift in perspective in hiring, as is the open communication with candidates, and among departments, that Schulze's initiative fostered. Developing a college-wide recognition of the depth of cultural change needed to transform a campus requires a commitment to such communication, as well as to collective decision-making processes.

It's important to note, of course, that a policy like SUNY's, enabling targeted hiring practices, is not available on many campuses. As a result, it might be easy to wave off Schulze's initiative as impossible elsewhere, as being dependent on that "secret sauce" to succeed. Yet it's worth considering how such a policy might similarly be developed and instantiated elsewhere. How might a coalition built from a council of deans, a provost, a university-level diversity and equity officer, and a president come together to present such a policy change to their board of trustees? How might that board be inspired to commit to such change and, where necessary, to promote it to the state?

This is an instance where something I ordinarily recoil from—universities' obsession with rankings—might be leveraged in our favor. As Schulze noted, "The AAU [Association of American Universities] talks all the time about the levels of representation inside the AAU [institutions]. At some point, when the schools that control the AAU are able to say, 'we have x percent representation,' they will flip a switch inside the AAU and say you have to have that level of representation to be a member. And that will be a game-changing moment. A bunch of schools will just fall right out." Our institutions are driven by rankings to compete all the time. How might we bring together a collective that insists to our institutions' governing bodies that we must become competitive in ways that really matter?

CHAPTER 18

Transforming Review

CHRISTOPHER P. LONG, CARA CILANO,
SONJA FRITZSCHE, BILL HART-DAVIDSON,
AND SCOTT SCHOPIERAY

Insofar as there's been a single most important influence in my thinking over the last several years about what leading generously might mean in the academic context, I'm lucky to be able to say that it's my own dean. Chris Long and his team in the College of Arts & Letters at MSU have focused much of their recent work around the idea that developing the faculty's and staff's abilities to tell rich, textured stories about our goals, as well as our abilities to read and interpret such stories, could enable the college to develop more generative and humane processes of evaluation along with better paths for career development for all of us. How to establish those paths and processes, however, isn't clear-cut—especially not in an environment conditioned by what a colleague has referred to as "the debilitating mathematics of prestige."[1] Our entrenched systems for personnel reviews suffer from that mathematics, as does everyone subject to them.

Part of the problem with the traditional measures we use in our reviews is their very mathematical nature. Reducing *what counts* in our evaluative processes to *what we can count*—as though "count" meant the same thing in these usages—eliminates many important ways that the impact of academic work can be imagined and take shape in the world. Our reliance on counting has admittedly come about, at least in part, for some good reasons: we strive to be as objective as we can in our evaluation processes, toward minimizing the effects of bias, by restricting our attention to things we can represent with empirical evidence. Somehow we've decided, though, that the most neutral form of empirical evidence is numerical, to the point where quantifying to compare things has become devastatingly naturalized.

But Long and his team have recognized that underlying this aspect of our broken processes of evaluation is a more fundamental inversion of ends and means: rather than examining the goals that we have for our work and our progress along the path toward them, we are instead laser-focused on a few specific stepping-stones on that path—the books, the grants, and the journal articles, notably—with the result being that these means have become ends in themselves.

Ensuring that we're reviewing the right things, for the right reasons and in the right ways, has been an ongoing project that Long has undertaken along with the college's associate and assistant deans, Cara Cilano, Sonja Fritzsche, Bill Hart-Davidson, and Scott Schopieray. Full disclosure requires that I say these are the folks who hired me, who support my work, and who review it regularly. My reviews have gone well, so it's possible that I'm suffering from confirmation bias; it's not unusual to find that you approve of people and processes that have had positive outcomes for you personally. But it's also important to say that I pursued the job that I'm in, reporting to and collaborating with this team of deans, in large part *because* of the work they have been doing to rethink the categories and purposes of evaluation.

Their project has come to be known within the college as CPIL, or Charting Pathways of Intellectual Leadership.[2] CPIL grew out of several different initiatives that were gradually connected. Chris Long, prior to joining MSU as dean, founded the *Public Philosophy Journal*, an experimental publication focused not only on doing philosophy in and with the public but also on transforming peer review from a summative, anonymous process into a formative, collaborative engagement between reviewers and authors that's intended to help the work take its strongest possible shape. Similarly, Bill Hart-Davidson, associate dean for research and graduate education, and Scott Schopieray, assistant dean for academic and research technology, collaborated on a series of workshops and initiatives designed to support members of the college in developing their digital presence and in imagining shapes for their scholarly outputs other than the book and the journal article.

What these precursors to CPIL share is the desire to create new means for members of the college to understand their goals and to shape their work with those goals in mind. Goal setting in the CPIL model asks everyone—not just the tenure-stream faculty but all faculty and staff—to begin by considering what success looks like for them, what they'd most want to be remembered for at the conclusion of their careers. Those longest-term goals are described as horizons, the things toward which one could spend a lifetime working, the purposes that keep that lifetime's work oriented. Along the way to those horizons, however, there are major milestones that need to be reached; those milestones, things like promotions, tend to be outside our direct control, but they can be prepared for through the stepping-stones of immediate work, the projects whose progress we can control.

Thinking about our intellectual pathways with this model reveals the extent to which our approach to evaluation and review has become bound up in accounting for the stepping-stones. We value publications, for instance, as if they were the goal, rather than recognizing them as merely steps along the way toward some larger horizon. As a result, we tend to count publications as indicators of performance and pay little or no attention to why these particular stepping-stones are the ones we've chosen or whether they are truly leading us toward the horizons we imagine.

Worse, because we have settled on the publication as a standard stepping-stone, we too often overlook the fact that we don't all share the same horizons. Where your vision of a successful career might be making a lasting contribution to the discourse of your field, mine might be building the systems and platforms through which others can make such contributions. And someone else's vision might center the desire to mentor the next generation of graduate students or to lift up a community through creative collaboration. Each of these visions can be a worthy horizon, but each requires different stepping-stones to create its path. When we restrict the forms that stepping-stones can take, we privilege the means over the ends, and we risk disqualifying the progress that others might make toward their own goals.

In fact, the very structure of faculty evaluation concretizes the ends/means error of reversal. The structures we use to describe academic work, and the forms we use to account for it, focus on the three traditional areas of research, teaching, and service, where each is weighted differently based on institutional goals. This tight focus on the means leading toward our ends produces real challenges for faculty whose end might look different from the usual expectations of their field. As Long described the situation,

> We were regularly encountering junior faculty in the tenure system coming to us with real concerns about how they were going to bring forward their research, teaching, and service

work in a holistic way that didn't require them to disentangle it and pull it apart into what felt like silos for them. A lot of this happened in conversations around, well, "our senior faculty colleagues are asking us to parse this work into . . . service and teaching. But you know our work is community based, and our teaching is bound up with the community work that we're doing. And so it doesn't even really make sense to pull them apart in that way." . . . That's not the conversation we wanted to be having, about what does this count as, what category does this fit into? We wanted to have a conversation about what's the purpose of the work? What's driving it, what's animating it, what are you trying to do with your academic life?[3]

This realization encouraged the deans to think about the ways they might describe the ends, the goals, that is, rather than the means by which they've traditionally been accomplished. They settled on three broad areas of academic endeavor, each of which reflects the overlaps among research, teaching, and service:

- Sharing knowledge
- Expanding opportunity
- Mentorship and stewardship

These areas are conditioned by the values that the college has named as defining the qualities it strives for in all its work, including equity, reciprocity, transparency, and creativity. Together, these areas, and the values that animate them, not only better correspond to the variety of horizons that anyone working in the college might establish for their work, but they also produce significant openness in the forms that the stepping-stones might take along the way to milestones like annual review or tenure and promotion.

194 | *The Stories*

For a model like this to produce the kinds of significant cultural change that the dean's team is seeking, however, has required a lot of education and encouragement. Sonja Fritzsche, associate dean of academic personnel and administration, noted that most people who work in the academy, when handed a rubric for assessment—even an expansive, values-enacted one—are conditioned to understand that rubric as a list of requirements. As a result, she found herself having conversations with directors of various units of the college who were struggling to understand how the work done by their teams fit the model: "they weren't feeling like they could have the freedom to think outside of this rubric or make it their own, because that has never been the culture." With deanly encouragement, however, to "take this and adapt it" to "make it your own," everyone within the college—faculty and staff alike, in every department or center or office—has been given room to develop their own leadership capacities, to think about the deep purposes of their work and the goals they're striving to reach, and to imagine how their daily activities can both better support them and be more supportively assessed.

Such adaptability, you might begin to suspect, threatens to transform what is now a uniformly applied process of evaluation and review into a highly individuated process, in which no two candidates can be assessed according to the same formula. That, as my friends in software development might say, is not a bug, but a feature: no two candidates have precisely the same goals for their work, or precisely the same methods of working, and no standardized system of review categories and credits can adequately account for the full range of their merits and accomplishments.

As a result, the college's evaluation processes have shifted significantly in their center of gravity. Every member of the faculty and staff is asked each year to develop a narrative that articulates their vision for themselves and their careers—the kinds of intellectual leadership that they would most like to embody—and then describes their near-term projects in light of this vision. This textured story enables supervisors and review committees and department chairs to understand more of the how and the why of an individual candidate's work than would focusing simply on its quantity. They are asked to treat the process as an opportunity for mentoring, by attending to the needs and goals of the person being reviewed and not to a standardized set of boxes to tick.

This process opens up room for a faculty member to make the case that their horizon is better served by publishing in public venues instead of scholarly ones or by participating in unexpected collaborations. It makes it possible for a staff member to describe their desire to obtain further professional development. It also encourages evaluators to keep an eye on how they can support that growth. Cara Cilano, then associate dean for undergraduate education, whose first encounters with the CPIL model came when she was chair of the English Department, explained that this individualized model transforms review from a hurdle to clear into "a punctuation mark in an ongoing conversation," one that allows evaluation "to be much more relational than transactional." That relationality rests on the bedrock of values that the college has collectively articulated for its work and continues to rearticulate, and it asks everyone to think about review as a personal engagement with their own dearest values and goals.

Implementing this model hasn't been simple, given everyone's inculturation in academic norms, and the deans recognize that there's still a lot of work in front of them. Not least of which is the "mentoring up" required to convince university-level administrators that they should approach their evaluation of the college using the same model. As Hart-Davidson noted, he recently received pointed questions from the vice-presidential level about why the college isn't producing the same number of books and articles as it had historically. His answer has been to point to the college's marked increase in other forms of work: award-winning documentary films, major exhibitions, successful digital projects, and significant grant funding. This work produces greater impact of the kind that a university espousing its commitments to its public mission should value.

After the university recognizes and begins to reward the kinds of values-enacted work being done within the college, there's yet another level of transformation still sought: revising the criteria for assessment and ranking of institutions done by organizations such as the Association of American Universities. But that transformation begins at this local level: the college has asked its personnel to move away from a quantitative evaluation process and toward one in which they tell a rich, textured story about the work they are doing and its significance for the life of the college. The college is likewise trying to tell its own textured story to the university administration. It follows, then, that universities will need to find ways to tell better stories about their work, its long-range purposes, and its cultural impact such that we can all begin to escape from the debilitating mathematics of prestige.

CHAPTER 19

Transforming Leadership

EDUCOPIA

Alongside my work as a member of the faculty of MSU, I am currently serving a three-year term (2022–2024) as the president of the board of directors of the Educopia Institute, a nonprofit organization focused on supporting communities that develop, share, and preserve knowledge both inside and outside the academy. Educopia is a values-enacted organization that strives for, among its other principles, "radical transparency coupled with reliability and responsiveness."[1]

Educopia was founded in 2006 by Katherine Skinner, executive director, and Martin Halbert, then board president, in order to provide administrative and strategic support for collaborations growing across the information management landscape. After 16 years as director, Skinner recognized that Educopia was at risk for a problem she'd observed in some communities she and her colleagues had assisted: "founder syndrome." She described it in a July 2022 blog post announcing her decision to step down: "Founder-led organizations often begin with visionary leaders who can marshal resources and create a safe, secure atmosphere that appeals to funders and community members. If founders stay too long, though, their organizations tend to become too reliant upon and too influenced by the founders' personalities, which can lead to stagnation and an unhealthy reciprocal dependence between the founder and the organization."[2]

Replacing a founder, however, and especially one as successful, respected, and, frankly, *loved* as Katherine Skinner, is no easy task. I count myself among those who love Katherine and who had a hard time imagining Educopia without her, and I admire beyond words the ethical conviction and organizational intelligence that led her to identify her apparent irreplaceability as the reason why the time had come for her to step down.

Skinner began planning for Educopia's leadership transition at least two years prior to her departure by thinking carefully about ways to share her knowledge with other members of the staff. Another crucial component of the transition was serious board development, as we would need a much different set of skills on the board to help support the organization into its next stage than we had on the board in the early days, when it functioned primarily as an advisory body supporting a talented and resourceful founder. We would need a much deeper understanding of the board's role in Educopia's governance, and we would also need to engage directly with the ethos of shared power that the Educopia team had embraced.

The board, in other words, needed to catch up with the staff as they worked to transition Educopia from a leader-centered startup into what Frederic Laloux would term a "Teal Organization," a purpose-driven nonprofit structured in ways that center equity and that enable and encourage leadership at every level. In order to do that work, we began a development process in which we plotted our own needs for growth at this moment of significant change, and we engaged Circle Forward, a consulting group helping organizations achieve "greater trust, equity, and resilience" in their governance processes.[3] Over several sessions with Circle

Forward principals Tracy Kunkler and Dee Washington, we considered what the role of the board of directors of an organization committed to equity and ethical collaboration should be and how the board could better support the work of the staff rather than governing from above.

In the course of that work, and as we considered Skinner's forthcoming departure, we gradually came to realize that Educopia might better be served by establishing shared leadership than by vesting leadership in a single executive; such a distribution of authority and responsibility might make the organization more resilient (and less subject to the turmoil of executive transition) in the years ahead. So, September 2022 ended with celebrations, both within Educopia and among its many friends, of the extraordinary work that Katherine Skinner had done over the years and with a warm welcome to its three amazing new codirectors: Jessica Meyerson, Katherine Kim, and Racquel Asante.[4] The codirectors were existing members of the Educopia team and thus had deep knowledge of the organization and its needs; they also bring balancing strengths to their codirection and are actively working to establish decision-making and communication processes that keep their work as open to the rest of the team as possible. The board continues to look for ways to support the codirectors and the whole team in this new leadership model, and I am honored to have the opportunity to collaborate with and learn from them in the process.

I want to hold up this story of Educopia's leadership transition as a counterpoint to the story of leadership turmoil I told in chapter 1, "Crisis." What have I carried away from my experience of two radically different leadership transitions, and what does the comparison mean for my ideas about the future of academic leadership? My thoughts from this are three.

One, that transparency is not just a good idea but an absolute necessity for organizations that are (or claim to be) "mission-driven." Without transparency there can be no trust, and without trust the people that make up the organization cannot sustain the level of care that the work requires.

Two, that while it's not often possible to plan for a leadership transition with the degree of thoughtfulness that Educopia managed, there are many ways to avoid plunging an institution into chaos by forcing a transition without any preparation. If an institution's governing board is going to uphold the values it claims to espouse, it must undertake transitions carefully and with respect for the many lives that will be affected in the process.

And three, that a leadership transition conceived and enacted as a means of sharing power, of creating collective strength, is radically different from one conceived and enacted as a means of coalescing power and of augmenting individual strength. One builds commitment. The other crushes it.

I originally wrote about these two leadership transitions in a blog post that opened with the first line of Charles Dickens's *A Tale of Two Cities*: "It was the best of times, it was the worst of times."[5] My choice of opening was flippant and cute, and yet the connection with the novel made me pause and reflect a bit, especially when I started thinking about how to end the post. For all the obvious reasons, I didn't want to close with Dickens's final words from the novel—"It is a far, far better thing that I do" was a bit much—but with his admonition from the beginning of the novel's final chapter. It struck close to home: "Crush humanity out of shape once more, under similar hammers, and it will twist itself into the same tortured forms. Sow the same seed of rapacious license and oppression over again, and it will surely yield the same fruit according to its kind."[6]

A damaging leadership transition isn't just damaging in the moment; it does lasting damage to the organization's ability to function, by twisting the relationships between the people who make up the organization and those who control it and ending up with tortured forms that cannot easily be reshaped. Repairing the relationships and recovering the organization requires change throughout, and nowhere more than in its governing structures and processes.

Such change is readily possible in small purpose-driven non-profits that are dedicated to creating and supporting collaborative communities. It's much, much harder to effect such structural change in an institution the size of a research university, at least without significant organizing and protest at all levels. The work of organizing, of building coalitions that can demand that our institutions of higher education become models of the new kinds of leadership the contemporary world needs, remains ahead.

PART IV

What's Next

CHAPTER 20

Onward

Ordinarily, this is where I would present a conclusion that fits together the pieces of what you've read in the preceding chapters. In the case of this book, however, concluding is hard: there isn't one overarching argument to be reiterated, and there isn't a definite outcome to be highlighted. It's all but impossible to conclude, after all, when the work is just beginning.

So what's called for here, at the end of this book, is less a conclusion than a benediction of sorts: a blessing (if a secular one) for your path ahead, because this is where I hand the project over to you and your collaborators. You know your on-the-ground situation far better than I ever could. You know where the opportunities for change lie, and where the resistance sits, and you know the colleagues you can work with to develop the best collection of ideas for moving forward.

So what remains for me to offer are a few words of advice for the road, things to bear in mind as you plan the work in front of you.

1. Start Small—but Think Big

The change we need in our institutions is enormous, and the thought of conceiving change on that scale can be paralyzing.

Melissa and Johnathan Nightingale describe being asked by a client about how to begin transforming the environment of work following COVID:

> *How do you know where to start? It's such a big, interrelated problem. How do you even begin?*
>
> And he's right. The individual boulders are enormous: the intersections of work and power and systematic oppression and burnout and isolation. We don't fault anyone for thinking they're hard to move. They are.
>
> But lifting boulders isn't about the giganticness. It's not about moving the whole thing in one go. It's about finding the places where movement can happen—the water flowing above, below, eroding the soil, chipping away until the entire landscape shifts.[1]

The places where movement can happen can be small, and they can be located anywhere on campus, in any office, with any project designed to make conditions better. These changes can be tightly local at the outset—and that scale can keep them manageable—but they can have ripple effects.

Even more importantly, small changes in multiple places, when coordinated, can gather to create something dramatic. So start with the immediate space around you and the things that most need repair. But talk with others about what you're doing and about the problems that they see, and think about how your projects might come together to transform a bigger landscape.

2. Be Patient—but Not Too Patient

Change is slow. Building coalitions is time-consuming work. Listening to those around you, trying hard to understand where they are coming from and what they need, and developing the trust necessary to working together—all of this requires deep patience and a willingness to take the time to put together something lasting.

That being said, as you know all too well, stalling is a time-honored practice of those resistant to change. Delays, slow-walking, and more and more meetings, these can serve as a means of thwarting those who are seeking to transform an institution, who are suffering under its status quo.

Finding the balance between patience and insistence can be a challenge. The goal is to maintain momentum and to ensure that you don't wear yourself and your colleagues out over the long haul. There will be progress, and there will be setbacks, and keeping focused throughout requires the right combination of hard work and stopping to breathe.

So be patient with yourself most of all. Recognize that you'll likely be learning how to navigate new systems and new relationships; such learning can be exhausting. Take some time to recharge in order to return to the work at full strength. This is not a delay; it's a necessity.

3. Be Prepared—but Stay Nimble

The terrain you're navigating has some features that are well known. There are undoubtedly processes for getting revised policies and structures approved that are familiar to you, such as how you get a proposal on a committee's agenda and where it goes from there. There are also personalities involved, people who are likely to respond to proposals in ways that are more or less predictable. Preparing for both the processes and the personalities is crucial.

You don't want to prepare so thoroughly, though, that you can't cope with sudden changes or take advantage of new opportunities as they present themselves. A new position may open, a new grant program may be announced—or, less obviously opportune on its face, a new crisis may draw attention to the need for change.

Remember the power involved in thinking about the need to adapt to circumstances not in terms of agility, or rapid movement for movement's sake, but in terms of nimbleness: accurately reading the path ahead and planning a course that will be successful. And remember that nimbleness and preparation go hand in hand: having a clear but flexible plan will let you keep an eye on the changing terrain.

4. Play the Long Game

It's easy to let short-term setbacks discourage you. It's also easy to let short-term wins make you comfortable. To avoid getting too caught up in immediate gains and losses, it's important to keep your eyes on the long term. Beware, though, as Carolyn Dever noted in my conversation with her, even leaders who "understand the long game" have a tendency to "get addicted to the quick win."[2] How can you ensure that the actions you're taking today are not just helping everyone through the current crisis but are helping to create a foundation for a better institution 10 years down the road?

Playing the long game—recognizing that some changes you make today won't pay off immediately and that some immediate improvements will have long-term costs—requires thinking strategically rather than tactically. Tactics are the expedient, on-the-ground moves you can make right away in striving for a goal. Tactics can be crucial, especially for creating change that begins outside conventional power structures, that grows from the grass-roots. But tactics can falter without a strategy to guide them and build upon them.

Strategic thinking requires a focus on long-term goals. Your strategy should describe the path to those goals; your tactics then become steps leading you along that path.

5. Work in the Environment You Want to Create

This piece of advice could be boiled down to "Be the Change": if you want to build an institution that is structurally capable of living up to its duty of care, you need to ensure that you're living up to that duty of care in the ways you go about transformation. That is to say, everything you do in the process of creating values-based policies and processes must itself be values-based. Building a more just world requires ensuring that justice is centered in your actions.

It sounds obvious. And yet it's awfully easy for movements toward change that are operating within hostile environments to bend to the ethos of those environments, where, for instance, a movement's desire for transparency and openness becomes infected by the secrecy and suspicion surrounding it.

Check in with yourself and your colleagues frequently. Remind yourselves why you're doing what you're doing. And explore ways that you can build a local environment that works the way you'd like the institution as a whole to work.

6. Take Care of Yourself as You Take Care of Others

It's all too easy for people committed to creating a better world to wear themselves out in the process. Transformational change is exhausting work, not least because of the obstacle course you're having to run, over and over. Your commitment can keep you going up to a point, but after that, burnout can set in, making even the smallest actions feel like trudging knee-deep through mud.

Taking time off—time to recuperate, time to re-center and re-ground—feels self-indulgent. It is not, though, a waste of time. In fact, attempting to power through when you're exhausted is counterproductive: you worsen your own exhaustion, because everything seems three times harder than it ought to be.

Finding means of self-care that help you maintain a sustainable commitment to the change you seek is a necessity. That might mean protecting your time away from work by shunning email and unplugging from the other ceaseless flows of networked demands. It might mean taking a few days off to focus on things that you find restorative. It might mean saying no to requests that don't help you further your goals.

The key here is to take care of yourself in the way you would try to take care of others around you.

7. Find—and Share—Other Guides and Sources of Support

This book and the tools it describes are more conceptual than practical. I haven't told you how to run your meetings or given you drafts for revised policies. Rather, my approach to thinking about leadership relies heavily on your own ideas as prompted by the issues and examples I discuss. What I suggest or describe won't work everywhere, though. You know your own situation and I don't. There are many other guides with different approaches that can help as well. The bibliography at the end of this book has some suggestions, but there are many others out there as well. I hope that you'll consider joining the Leading Generously group at Humanities Commons and that you'll share your favorite resources there.

Acknowledgments

Every book is an act of collaboration; to say that this book is somehow more so than others is not to point to its particular virtues (and especially not any virtues of its author) but rather to the remarkable generosity of the community that supported me in the process of writing and especially revising it. My collaborators in this process of course include the endlessly patient and encouraging Greg Britton, the thorough and insightful Robert Brown, and the enthusiastic and caring Kris Lykke at Hopkins Press. I also owe a debt of gratitude to the anonymous reviewers of the book proposal; their generous critique pushed me to think hard about my reasons and methods for this project, in particular urging me to talk with leaders who had more experience in the higher reaches of university administration than I did. I owe a similar debt to the anonymous reviewer of the full manuscript, who pushed me to think outside my own frame of reference and include folks struggling on the institutional front lines.

The resulting interviews were among the most exciting research experiences I've ever had. I found it both energizing and inspiring to spend time talking with brilliant, committed folks who shared their stories and thought with me about what they might mean for the future of leadership in higher education. Huge thanks to Helen Berry, Beth Bouloukos, Chris Bourg, Sayeed Choudhury, Carolyn Dever, Eric Elliott, Greg Eow, Dianne Harris, George Justice, Evviva Weinraub Lajoie, Benjamin Lowenkron, Shannon Miller, Trevor Owens, Este Pope, Robin Schulze, Katherine Skinner, and the three interviewees who asked to remain anonymous. Their insights, their excitement, and their time proved invaluable to pushing this project forward.

I also want to thank the folks who led the leadership workshops I had an opportunity to participate in during the research and writing process: Ari Weinzweig and Maggie Bayless of ZingTrain and Johnathan Nightingale and Melissa Nightingale of Raw Signal Group. Their care and creativity in imagining the kinds of support that purpose-driven leaders might require—especially through the turmoil of recent years—has proven a sustaining inspiration.

Anne Khademian invited me to spend several days visiting the campuses of Virginia Tech in 2019. During the drive between one and another of those campuses, she suggested that I think about a follow-up to *Generous Thinking*; I don't know that this volume is exactly what she had in mind, but that conversation set me on the path. Thanks are due as well to the colleagues who invited me to give a number of talks in which I worked out various pieces of this project, including Joshua Billings at Princeton University, Robin DeRosa at Plymouth State University, Michelle Miley at Montana State University, Jacqueline Reich at Marist College, Ray Siemens and Alyssa Arbuckle at the University of Victoria, Alexander Starre at the Freie Universität Berlin, and Janine Utell at the Modern Language Association. Your hospitality, when we were able to talk in person, and your warm Zoom presence when we couldn't, were a key form of support in the process.

I also want to thank the readers who participated in the open review I hosted on Humanities Commons in August 2022. These readers paid careful attention to the manuscript in its second-draft state, sharing their thoughts and concerns in ways that were invaluable to me as I revised. Thanks to Martin Paul Eve, Anke Finger, Sonja Fritzsche, Shawn Graham, Eileen Joy, Rebecca Kennison, François Lachance, Katina Rogers, Dorothea Salo, and Janine Utell.

Thanks go as well to the amazing leaders that I have the privilege of working with at Michigan State University, including Chris Long, Bill Hart-Davidson, Sonja Fritzsche, and Scott Schopieray in the Dean's Office of the College of Arts & Letters at MSU; Justus Nieland, Kristin Mahoney, Cara Cilano, and too many other excellent colleagues to name in the English Department; as well as Kristen Mapes, Kate Topham, and Max Evjen in DH@MSU.

Above all, I want to thank the amazing people who have come to work with me in Mesh Research. We have spent the last couple of years not just working on our tools and platforms but working on the team, keeping an explicit focus on the ways we work together and the values that underwrite everything we do. For their enthusiasm, their care, and their commitment to a more open, more collaborative, more ethical, and more diverse global knowledge community, I am endlessly grateful to Brian Adams, Larissa Babak, Brian Boggan, Shelby Brewster, Grant Eben, Nicole Huff, Katie Knowles, Titi Kou-Herrema, Kristen Lee, Cassandra Lem, Annabelle Miller, Christine Peffer, Bonnie Russell, Kelly Sattler, Scott Schopieray, Ian Scott, Michael Thicke, Dimitris Tzouris, Stephanie Vasko, Shel Vilag, and Zoe Wake Hyde. You embody generous leadership, one and all.

Notes

Introduction

1. Brim, *Poor Queer Studies*, 12–13.
2. Utell, "Thinking about Two Things Here . . ."
3. Boyer, "Building the New."
4. McMillan Cottom, "That Is a Pretty Impolitic Stance . . ."
5. A nakedly hierarchical term that I'd really like to see us break ourselves of.
6. Solnit, *Hope in the Dark*.
7. Fitzpatrick, *Generous Thinking*, xii.
8. T. Snyder, *On Tyranny*, 12.

Chapter 1. Crisis

1. Reiter and Wellmon, *Permanent Crisis*, 132.
2. National Center for Education Statistics, "Characteristics of Post-secondary Students."
3. "Tenure" is a relatively US-centric notion; many other nations' higher education systems do not have this particular structure of job security provided after the successful completion of a probationary period and review. Those systems, such as that in the United Kingdom, often do have, however, a similarly hierarchical structure of professorial ranks accompanied by a range of benefits. Where I use "tenure" in this book, I hope you'll take it to include these other structures as well.
4. Perkins, "While Governor, John Engler Fought Hard against Prison Sex Abuse Victims."
5. Jesse, "Sources."
6. See, for instance, the statement released by the Association of American Universities: B. Snyder, "AAU President Expresses Deep Concern about Michigan State University Trustees' Interference in School Operations."
7. Johnson and Bolanos, "Michigan State President Samuel Stanley Resigns, Cites Loss of Confidence in Board."
8. Stripling and Svrluga, "Colleges Want Open Doors."
9. The State News Editorial Board, "EDITORIAL."
10. Gibbons and Lohman, "'We're So Angry.'"
11. The *Daily Tar Heel* noted that Guskiewicz "faced possible termination after the UNC BOT denied Hannah-Jones tenure in 2021" and that he also faced questions about his involvement in the university's settlement with a chapter of the Sons of Confederate Veterans over the removal of the Silent Sam monument on campus (Pender and Quincin, "As Guskiewicz Considers Departure"). Additionally, in fall 2023, the North Carolina legislature passed a budget that disallowed

the use of state funds for distinguished professorships at public universities in fields outside science, technology, engineering, and mathematics (Quinn, "New State-Funded N.C. Distinguished Professorships Will Be Limited to STEM"). It is no doubt that these experiences, coupled with Guskiewicz's attention to MSU's recent history, led him to sign an agreement with the MSU board of trustees defining the governance principles under which they would work together (Board of Trustees, "Board of Trustees Signs Commitments around Governance Principles with MSU President-Elect").

12. See Allison, Misra, and Perry, "Doing More with More"; Mont, "The Future of Nonprofit Leadership"; and Duncan et al., "Butterflies, Pads, and Pods," just to name a few.
13. Laloux, *Reinventing Organizations*, 250.
14. Spade, *Mutual Aid*.
15. Kropotkin, *Mutual Aid*, 296.

Chapter 2. Leadership
1. Harris, "Interview."
2. Eve, "Just a Rhetorical Question . . ."
3. It's of course just as important to note that many of our bad ideas about leadership likewise fester in and emanate from business schools.
4. Kotter, "What Leaders Really Do," 38.
5. Kotter, 37.
6. Kezar, *How Colleges Change*, xiii–xvi.
7. Senge, *The Fifth Discipline*, 319.
8. Senge, xvii–xviii.
9. Schein and Schein, *Humble Inquiry*, xiii.
10. Harris, "Interview."
11. Hass, *A Leadership Guide for Women in Higher Education*, 95.
12. Heifetz and Laurie, "The Work of Leadership," 77.
13. Andre, *Lead for the Planet*, 3.
14. Bozeman and Crow, *Public Values Leadership*, 54.
15. brown, *Emergent Strategy*, 64.
16. Choudhury, "Interview."
17. Montgomery, *Lessons from Plants*, 149.
18. Ancona et al., "In Praise of the Incomplete Leader," 179.
19. Ancona et al., 187.
20. McMillan Cottom, *Lower Ed*, 182.
21. In fact, Matt Brim's *Poor Queer Studies* encourages us to consider whether it's the inequities that are keeping us stuck or whether we are in fact recreating the inequities over and over again through our processes of institutional formation.
22. Young, *Justice and the Politics of Difference*, 9.
23. Young, 34.

24. Eve, "As Before . . ."
25. Lajoie, "Interview."
26. Young, *Justice and the Politics of Difference*, 69.
27. Young, 69.
28. Young, 211.
29. Táíwò, *Elite Capture*, 12–13.
30. Fitzpatrick, *Planned Obsolescence*.
31. Young, *Justice and the Politics of Difference*, 79.
32. Kennison, "Back to the Future."
33. Young, *Justice and the Politics of Difference*, 77.
34. Respondent 15, "Interview."
35. Lajoie, "Interview."

Chapter 3. People
1. Senge, *The Fifth Discipline*, 268.
2. Ahmed, *Living a Feminist Life*.
3. Eve, "A Question Occurred to Me . . ."
4. Nightingale and Nightingale, *Unmanageable*, 67.
5. Kennison, "While I Like This Quote a Lot . . ."
6. Ettarh, "Vocational Awe and Librarianship."
7. See, as just two among many possible references, Jayasinghe, "Avoiding Burnout and Preserving Movement Leadership," and Morrissette, "Five Myths That Perpetuate Burnout across Nonprofits."
8. Shaw, *The Greater Good*, 199.
9. Daniels, "A Message from President Daniels regarding Fall Semester."
10. White, "Message from the Office of the Chancellor."
11. This is not a wasted effort in an era when politicians seem determined to tear those institutions down. See Timothy Snyder: "It is institutions that help us to preserve decency. They need our help as well. Do not speak of 'our institutions' unless you make them yours by acting on their behalf. Institutions do not protect themselves. They fall one after another unless each is defended from the beginning" (*On Tyranny*, 12).
12. Marshall Sahlins explores the particular ends-means inversion that derives from an emphasis on revenue, noting that for all his critiques of the governing structure of universities, Thorstein Veblen "did not foresee the day when money ceased to be merely the means of making the university, but more and more the university became the means of making money—a development consummated in today's for-profit institutions, yet long prefigured in the best research universities" ("The Conflicts of the Faculty," 1002).

Chapter 4. Yourself
1. Weinzweig, *A Lapsed Anarchist's Approach to Being a Better Leader*, 259.
2. Weinzweig, 265.

3. Rogers, "In Some Ways It's a Discrepancy . . ."
4. Baldwin, *Collected Essays*, 738.
5. Kennison, "This Is the First Step . . ."

Chapter 5. Vulnerability
1. Lajoie, "Interview."
2. Schein and Schein, *Humble Inquiry*, 18.
3. Zimmerman, "Why Is Male Anger So Threatening?"
4. Brown, *Dare to Lead*, 36.
5. Elliott and Lowenkron, "Interview."
6. Respondent 14, "Interview."
7. Buss, "An Introduction," 10.
8. Fritzsche, "Disagreement Is an Opportunity . . ."
9. Harris, "Interview."
10. Elliott and Lowenkron, "Interview."
11. Heifetz and Laurie, "The Work of Leadership," 69.
12. Schulze, "Interview."
13. Salo, "Hm. Yes . . ."
14. Costa and Kallick, "Through the Lens of a Critical Friend," 50.

Chapter 6. Together
1. Bourg, "Interview."
2. MIT Libraries, "MIT Framework for Publisher Contracts."
3. Caiazza, "So You Want to Climb the Org Chart?" Thanks to Rebecca Kennison for this reference.
4. Valamis, "Shared Leadership."
5. Laloux, *Reinventing Organizations*, 89.
6. Buss, "An Introduction," 14.
7. Skinner, "Interview."
8. Respondent 5, "Interview."
9. Senge, *The Fifth Discipline*, 192.
10. Berry, "Interview."
11. Spade, *Mutual Aid*.
12. Berry, "Interview."
13. Pope, "Interview."

Chapter 7. Trust
1. Choudhury, "Interview."
2. Feltman, *The Thin Book of Trust*.
3. Laloux, *Reinventing Organizations*, 148.
4. Feltman, *The Thin Book of Trust*.
5. Respondent 5, "Interview."
6. Schulze, "Interview."
7. Long et al., "Interview."

8. Kennison, "This Is the First Step . . ."
9. Stack with Burlingham, *The Great Game of Business*.
10. Stack with Burlingham.
11. Skinner, "Interview."
12. Kennison, "While I Like This Quote a Lot . . ."
13. Spade, *Mutual Aid*.
14. Spade.
15. Lachance, "Record Keeping . . ."
16. GitLab, "The Importance of a Handbook-First Approach to Documentation."
17. GitLab, "GitLab's Guide to All-Remote."
18. Feltman, *The Thin Book of Trust*.

Chapter 8. Values
1. See, for instance, Blum, *Ungrading*, and Nilson, *Specifications Grading*.
2. Bouloukos, "Interview."
3. Embedded in this narrative is another lesson about the power of accrediting bodies and whether it is always appropriately wielded and to what end. But that's an argument for another book.
4. Young, *Justice and the Politics of Difference*, 79.
5. Laloux, *Reinventing Organizations*, 224.
6. HuMetrics HSS, "Walking the Talk," 8.
7. HuMetrics HSS, 6.
8. Rhody, "On 'The Value of Values' Workshop."
9. HuMetrics HSS, "Walking the Talk," 7.
10. HuMetrics HSS, 11.
11. See Fitzpatrick, *Planned Obsolescence*, for much, much more on rethinking peer review.
12. Owens, "Interview."

Chapter 9. Listening
1. Schein and Schein, *Humble Inquiry*, x.
2. Bouloukos, "Interview." I have to note: this moment in our interview made me wince in retrospective embarrassment; her description of charging in and telling everyone they're doing it wrong reminded me all too much of several of the presentations I'd given for her colleagues back in the day. Then again, I'd been invited to speak in order to provoke discussion, so provocation was the order of the day, I guess.
3. Schein and Schein, *Humble Inquiry*, 3.
4. Elliott and Lowenkron, "Interview."
5. Tsing, *The Mushroom at the End of the World*, 254.
6. Hochschild, *Strangers in Their Own Land*.
7. Dever, "Interview."
8. Owens, "Interview."

Chapter 10. Transparency

1. Spade, *Mutual Aid*.
2. Laloux, *Reinventing Organizations*, 137.
3. See Ahmed, *Living a Feminist Life*.
4. See Stack with Burlingham, *The Great Game of Business*.
5. On the gory underside of university budgeting, see Newfield, *The Great Mistake*.
6. My qualifier in this sentence, "at least not yet," has a footnote: it has been known within the university for the last couple of years that our budget model will be changing, but exactly how so is not yet clear. We have been told that it will not be pure RCM, or responsibility center management, but we haven't been told much more. These gaps in communication, perhaps needless to say, are not inspiring trust.

Chapter 11. Nimbleness

1. On the history of agile and its effects on work cultures, see Posner, "Agile and the Long Crisis of Software."
2. Owens, "Interview."
3. Elliott and Lowenkron, "Interview."
4. Kezar, *How Colleges Change*, 19.
5. Vise and Kumar, "U-Va. Board Leaders Wanted President Teresa Sullivan to Make Cuts."
6. Rice, "Anatomy of a Campus Coup."
7. Vise and Kumar, "U-Va. Board Leaders Wanted President Teresa Sullivan to Make Cuts."
8. Chafkin, "Udacity's Sebastian Thrun, Godfather of Free Online Education, Changes Course."
9. On that corporate hubris, see Taplin, *Move Fast and Break Things*. On values related to the public good, see Bozeman and Crow, *Public Values Leadership*.
10. Warzel and Petersen, *Out of Office*.
11. American Association of University Professors, "Data Snapshot."
12. Nowviskie, "Design—and Sustain!—Resilient Systems."
13. Miller, "Interview."
14. "Nimble," adj.; "Agile," adj.
15. "Nimble," adj., adv., and n.
16. On the changes needed in graduate programs, see Cassuto and Weisbuch, *The New PhD*, and Rogers, *Putting the Humanities PhD to Work*.
17. Hall, *The Uberfication of the University*.
18. Eve, "I Really Like This . . ."

Chapter 12. Narrative

1. See Settles et al., "Epistemic Exclusion," on the ways that exclusion is aided by disciplinary norms such as objectivity.
2. Young, *Justice and the Politics of Difference*, 9.

3. See, as just one recent example, Kim, "Harvard Professor Who Studies Dishonesty Is Accused of Falsifying Data."
4. See the work of the Association of Science Communicators, "Association of Science Communicators—Giving Science a Voice."
5. Sahlins, "The Conflicts of the Faculty," 1009–10.

Chapter 13. Sustainability
1. Association for the Advancement of Sustainability in Higher Education, "STARS, Sustainability Tracking Assessment & Rating System."
2. Berlant, *Cruel Optimism*.
3. Newfield, *The Great Mistake*.
4. Choudhury, "Interview."
5. Ostrom, *Governing the Commons*, 6–7.
6. Katopodis, "Teaching for a Habitable Future with Octavia Butler's *Parable of the Sower*," 82.

Chapter 14. Solidarity
1. Joseph, *Against the Romance of Community*.
2. Kendall, *Hood Feminism*, 3.
3. Kendall, 7.
4. Respondent 15, "Interview."
5. Justice, *How to Be a Dean*, 81.
6. This kind of resistance is hardly unusual, and it extends well beyond labor relations. As Beth Bouloukos discussed her work to promote open access publishing with me, she noted her surprise at finding "that others with a lot more power, and a lot more money and a lot more prestige, can be really threatened by you, and really threatened by change" (Bouloukos, "Interview").
7. Bradbury, *Secrets of a Successful Organizer*, 4.
8. Justice, "Interview."

Chapter 15. Transforming Institutional Structure
1. MIT Libraries, "Meet Chris Bourg."
2. Hartman, "Greg Eow Named Associate Director for Collections of MIT Libraries."
3. This and all other quotations from Greg Eow in this chapter come from Eow, "Interview."
4. Kennison, "Is It Worth Mentioning . . ."

Chapter 16. Transforming Community
1. Baton Rouge Community College, "Faculty Workload."
2. This and all other quotations for Eric Elliott or Benjamin Lowenkron in this chapter derive from Elliott and Lowenkron, "Interview."
3. United States Department of Education, "Predominantly Black Institutions Program—Formula Grants."

4. This reliance on "broad shoulders" turns out to be a poor strategy for sustaining key initiatives, as became evident when Lowenkron announced while this book was in press that he would be leaving BRCC after 14 years to take up a position with the Louisiana Community & Technical College System.

Chapter 17. Transforming Hiring
1. Lajoie, "Interview."
2. This and all quotations that follow in this story derive from Schulze, "Interview."

Chapter 18. Transforming Review
1. I owe this phrase to Chuck Henry, president of CLIR, who used it during a discussion about university ranking systems, but the mathematics involved, and the categorical mistakes it relies on, are fractal, strangling higher education from the institutional to the individual, and at every level in between.
2. Fritzsche, Hart-Davidson, and Long, "Charting Pathways of Intellectual Leadership."
3. This and all quotations that follow in this story derive from Long et al., "Interview."

Chapter 19. Transforming Leadership
1. Educopia Institute, "About."
2. Skinner, "Embracing Change."
3. Circle Forward, "Circle Forward | #Collaborativegovernance."
4. Asante, Kim, and Meyerson, "Introducing Our Shared Leadership Model."
5. Fitzpatrick, "A Tale of Two Transitions."
6. Dickens, *A Tale of Two Cities*.

Chapter 20. Onward
1. Nightingale and Nightingale, *Unmanageable*, 147.
2. Dever, "Interview."

Bibliography

"Agile," adj. *Merriam-Webster Online*. Accessed March 3, 2022.

Ahmed, Sara. *Living a Feminist Life*. Duke University Press, 2017.

Allison, Michael, Susan Misra, and Elissa Perry. "Doing More with More: Putting Shared Leadership into Practice." *Nonprofit Quarterly*, June 2018.

American Association of University Professors. "Data Snapshot: Contingent Faculty in US Higher Ed." AAUP, October 2018. https://www.aaup.org/news/data-snapshot-contingent-faculty-us-higher-ed.

Ancona, Deborah, Thomas W. Malone, Wanda J. Orlikowski, and Peter M. Senge. "In Praise of the Incomplete Leader." In *HBR's 10 Must Reads on Leadership*, 179–96. Harvard Business Review Press, 2011.

Andre, Rae. *Lead for the Planet: Five Practices for Confronting Climate Change*. Aevo UTP, 2020.

Asante, Raquel, Katherine Kim, and Jessica Meyerson. "Introducing Our Shared Leadership Model." Educopia Institute, September 2022. https://educopia.org/introducing-our-shared-leadership-model/.

Association for the Advancement of Sustainability in Higher Education. "STARS, Sustainability Tracking Assessment & Rating System." Accessed June 22, 2022. https://stars.aashe.org/.

Association of Science Communicators. "Association of Science Communicators—Giving Science a Voice." June 2023. https://www.associationofsciencecommunicators.org/.

Baldwin, James. "A Report from Occupied Territory." *1966. In Collected Essays*. Library of America, 1998.

Baton Rouge Community College. "Faculty Workload: Policy 1.7060." May 13, 2021. https://www.mybrcc.edu/about-brcc/policy-index/academic_affairs_policy/policies/1_7060FacultyWorkloadPolicy20210519.pdf.

Berlant, Lauren. *Cruel Optimism*. Duke University Press, 2011.

Berry, Helen. "Interview." May 2021.

Blum, Susan Debra, ed. *Ungrading: Why Rating Students Undermines Learning (and What to Do Instead)*. West Virginia University Press, 2020.

Board of Trustees, Michigan State University. "Board of Trustees Signs Commitments around Governance Principles with MSU President-Elect." 2023. https://trustees.msu.edu/communications/board-statements/2023-statements/2023-12-13-2023-governance%20principles.html.

Bouloukos, Beth. "Interview." April 2021.

Bourg, Chris. "Interview." May 2021.

Boyer, Rich. "Building the New." Great Colleges to Work For 2022. https://greatcollegesprogram.com/list/article.

Bozeman, Barry, and Michael M. Crow. *Public Values Leadership: Striving to Achieve Democratic Ideals*. Johns Hopkins University Press, 2021.

Bradbury, Alexandra. *Secrets of a Successful Organizer*. Labor Notes, 2016.

Brim, Matt. *Poor Queer Studies: Confronting Elitism in the University*. Duke University Press, 2020.

brown, adrienne maree. *Emergent Strategy: Shaping Change, Changing Worlds*. AK Press, 2017.

Brown, Brené. *Dare to Lead: Brave Work. Tough Conversations. Whole Hearts.* Random House, 2018.

Buss, Sarah. "An Introduction." In *Radical Humility: Essays on Ordinary Acts*, edited by Rebekah Modrak and Jamie Vander Broek, 9–15. Belt Publishing, 2021.

Caiazza, Matthew. "So You Want to Climb the Org Chart?" *Medium*, March 2020.

Cassuto, Leonard, and Robert Weisbuch. *The New PhD: How to Build a Better Graduate Education*. Johns Hopkins University Press, 2021.

Chafkin, Max. "Udacity's Sebastian Thrun, Godfather of Free Online Education, Changes Course." *Fast Company*, November 2013. https://www.fastcompany.com/3021473/udacity-sebastian-thrun-uphill-climb.

Choudhury, Sayeed. "Interview." June 2022.

Circle Forward. "Circle Forward | #Collaborativegovernance." Accessed June 14, 2023. https://circleforward.us/.

Costa, Arthur L., and Bena Kallick. "Through the Lens of a Critical Friend." *Educational Leadership* 51, no. 2 (October 1993): 49–51.

Daniels, Mitchell E., Jr. "A Message from President Daniels regarding Fall Semester." Office of the President, Purdue University, April 2020. https://www.purdue.edu/president/messages/campus-community/2020/2004-fall-message.php.

Dever, Carolyn. "Interview." March 2021.

Dickens, Charles. *A Tale of Two Cities*. 1859. Project Gutenberg, 2021.

Duncan, Aja Couchois, Mark Leach, Elissa Sloan Perry, and Natasha Winegar. "Butterflies, Pads, and Pods: Interdependent Leadership for the World We Want." Change Elemental, October 2021.

Educopia Institute. "About." Accessed June 14, 2023. https://educopia.org/about/.

Elliott, Eric, and Benjamin Lowenkron. "Interview." October 2023.

Eow, Greg. "Interview." April 2021.

Ettarh, Fobazi. "Vocational Awe and Librarianship: The Lies We Tell Ourselves." *In the Library with the Lead Pipe*, January 2018.

Eve, Martin Paul. "As Before . . ." Comment on "Leading Generously," Humanities Commons, August 2022.

———. "I Really Like This . . ." Comment on "Leading Generously," Humanities Commons, August 2022.

———. "Just a Rhetorical Question . . ." Comment on "Leading Generously," Humanities Commons, August 2022.

———. "A Question Occurred to Me . . ." Comment on "Leading Generously," Humanities Commons, August 2022.

Feltman, Charles. *The Thin Book of Trust*. Thin Book Publishing, 2021.

Fitzpatrick, Kathleen. *Generous Thinking*. Johns Hopkins University Press, 2019.

———. *Planned Obsolescence: Publishing, Technology, and the Future of the Academy*. New York University Press, 2011.

———. "A Tale of Two Transitions." *Kathleen Fitzpatrick*, October 2022. https://kfitz.info/a-tale-of-two-transitions/.

Fritzsche, Sonja. "Disagreement Is an Opportunity . . ." Comment on "Leading Generously," Humanities Commons, October 2022.

Fritzsche, Sonja, William Hart-Davidson, and Christopher P. Long. "Charting Pathways of Intellectual Leadership: An Initiative for Transformative Personal and Institutional Change." *Change: The Magazine of Higher Learning* 54, no. 3 (May 2022): 19–27. https://doi.org/10.1080/00091383.2022.2054175.

Gibbons, Lauren, and Isabel Lohman. "'We're So Angry.' MSU Students Urge Gun Safety at Lansing Hearing." Bridge Michigan, March 2023.

GitLab. "GitLab's Guide to All-Remote." GitLab, n.d. https://about.gitlab.com/company/culture/all-remote/guide/.

———. "The Importance of a Handbook-First Approach to Documentation." GitLab, n.d. https://about.gitlab.com/company/culture/all-remote/handbook-first-documentation/.

Hall, Gary. *The Uberfication of the University*. University of Minnesota Press, 2016.

Harris, Dianne. "Interview." March 2021.

Hartman, Stephanie. "Greg Eow Named Associate Director for Collections of MIT Libraries." *MIT Libraries News*, n.d. https://libraries.mit.edu/news/named-associate-director/19220/.

Hass, Marjorie. *A Leadership Guide for Women in Higher Education*. Johns Hopkins University Press, 2021.

Heifetz, Ronald A., and Donald L. Laurie. "The Work of Leadership." In *HBR's 10 Must Reads on Leadership*, 57–78. Harvard Business Review Press, 2011.

Hochschild, Arlie Russell. *Strangers in Their Own Land: Anger and Mourning on the American Right*. New Press, 2016.

HuMetrics HSS. "Walking the Talk: Toward a Values-Aligned Academy." February 2022.

Jayasinghe, Tiloma. "Avoiding Burnout and Preserving Movement Leadership." *Nonprofit Quarterly*, July 2021.

Jesse, Davis. "Sources: MSU Board Gives School President until Tuesday to Agree to Step Down." *Detroit Free Press*, September 2022.

Johnson, Mark, and Veronica Bolanos. "Michigan State President Samuel Stanley Resigns, Cites Loss of Confidence in Board." *Lansing State Journal*, October 2022.

Joseph, Miranda. *Against the Romance of Community*. University of Minnesota Press, 2002.

Justice, George. *How to Be a Dean*. Johns Hopkins University Press, 2019.

———. "Interview." February 2021.

Katopodis, Christina. "Teaching for a Habitable Future with Octavia Butler's *Parable of the Sower.*" *English Language Notes* 61, no. 1 (April 2023): 77–94. https://doi.org/10.1215/00138282-10293184.

Kendall, Mikki. *Hood Feminism: Notes from the Women That a Movement Forgot*. Viking, 2020.

Kennison, Rebecca. "Back to the Future: (Re)turning from Peer Review to Peer Engagement." *Learned Publishing* 29, no. 1 (2016): 69–71. https://doi.org/10.1002/leap.1001.

———. "Is It Worth Mentioning . . ." Comment on "Leading Generously," Humanities Commons, August 2022.

———. "So Is, I Think . . ." Comment on "Leading Generously," Humanities Commons, August 2022.

———. "This Is the First Step . . ." Comment on "Leading Generously," Humanities Commons, August 2022.

———. "While I Like This Quote a Lot . . ." Comment on "Leading Generously," Humanities Commons, August 2022.

———. "Your Observation Above . . ." Comment on "Leading Generously," Humanities Commons, August 2022.

Kezar, Adrianna. *How Colleges Change: Understanding, Leading, and Enacting Change*. 2nd ed. Routledge, 2014.

Kim, Juliana. "Harvard Professor Who Studies Dishonesty Is Accused of Falsifying Data." NPR, sec. Education, June 26, 2023. https://www.npr.org/2023/06/26/1184289296/harvard-professor-dishonesty-francesca-gino.

Kotter, John P. "What Leaders Really Do." In *HBR's 10 Must Reads on Leadership*, 37–55. Harvard Business Review Press, 2011.

Kropotkin, Petr Alekseevich. *Mutual Aid: A Factor of Evolution*. William Heineman, 1902.

Lachance, François. "Record Keeping . . ." Comment on "Leading Generously," Humanities Commons, August 2022.

Lajoie, Evviva Weinraub. "Interview." May 2021.

Laloux, Frédéric. *Reinventing Organizations: A Guide to Creating Organizations Inspired by the Next Stage of Human Consciousness*. Nelson Parker, 2014.

Long, Christopher P., Sonja Fritzsche, William Hart-Davidson, Cara Cilano, and Scott Schopieray. "Interview." March 2022.

McMillan Cottom, Tressie. *Lower Ed: The Troubling Rise of For-Profit Colleges in the New Economy*. New Press, 2017.

———. "That Is a Pretty Impolitic Stance . . ." *Twitter*, February 2020.

Miller, Shannon. "Interview." March 2021.

MIT Libraries. "Meet Chris Bourg." *MIT Libraries News*, n.d. https://libraries.mit.edu/news/bibliotech/chris-bourg/.

———. "MIT Framework for Publisher Contracts." Scholarly Publishing—MIT Libraries, n.d. https://libraries.mit.edu/scholarly/publishing/framework/.

Mont, Simon. "The Future of Nonprofit Leadership: Worker Self-Directed Organizations." *Nonprofit Quarterly*, March 2017.

Montgomery, Beronda L. *Lessons from Plants*. Harvard University Press, 2021.

Morrissette, Ann-Sophie. "Five Myths That Perpetuate Burnout across Nonprofits." *Stanford Social Innovation Review*, October 2016.

National Center for Education Statistics. "Characteristics of Postsecondary Students." August 2023. https://nces.ed.gov/programs/coe/indicator/csb.

Newfield, Christopher. *The Great Mistake: How We Wrecked Public Universities and How We Can Fix Them*. Johns Hopkins University Press, 2016.

Nightingale, Johnathan, and Melissa Nightingale. *Unmanageable: Leadership Lessons from an Impossible Year*. Raw Signal Press, 2021.

Nilson, Linda Burzotta. *Specifications Grading: Restoring Rigor, Motivating Students, and Saving Faculty Time*. Stylus Publishing, 2015.

"Nimble," adj. *Merriam-Webster Online*. Accessed March 3, 2022.

"Nimble," adj., adv., and n. *OED Online*. Accessed March 3, 2022.

Nowviskie, Bethany. "Design—and Sustain!—Resilient Systems." *Twitter*, April 2022.

Ostrom, Elinor. *Governing the Commons: The Evolution of Institutions for Collective Action*. Cambridge University Press, 1990.

Owens, Trevor. "Interview." March 2021.

Pender, Abby, and Ashley Quincin. "As Guskiewicz Considers Departure, Some Faculty Are Concerned over Possible Destabilization." *Daily Tar Heel,* November 29, 2023. https://www.dailytarheel.com/article/2023/11/university-what-we-know-about-kevin-guskiewicz.

Perkins, Tom. "While Governor, John Engler Fought Hard against Prison Sex Abuse Victims." *Detroit Metro Times*, February 2018.

Pope, Este. "Interview." February 2021.

Posner, Miriam. "Agile and the Long Crisis of Software." *Logic*, no. 16 (2022).

Quinn, Ryan. "New State-Funded N.C. Distinguished Professorships Will Be Limited to STEM." Inside Higher Ed, October 30, 2023. https://www.insidehighered.com/news/faculty-issues/career-development/2023/10/30/new-state-funded-nc-distinguished-professorships.

Reitter, Paul, and Chad Wellmon. *Permanent Crisis: The Humanities in a Disenchanted Age*. University of Chicago Press, 2021.

Respondent 5. "Interview." March 2021.

Respondent 14. "Interview." June 2021.

Respondent 15. "Interview." September 2021.

Rhody, Jason. "On 'The Value of Values' Workshop." HuMetrics HSS, November 2017.

Rice, Andrew. "Anatomy of a Campus Coup." *New York Times*, September 2012.

Rogers, Katina. "In Some Ways It's a Discrepancy . . ." Comment on "Leading Generously," Humanities Commons, September 2022.

———. *Putting the Humanities PhD to Work: Thriving in and beyond the Classroom.* Duke University Press, 2020.

Sahlins, Marshall. "The Conflicts of the Faculty." *Critical Inquiry* 35 (2009): 997–1017.

Salo, Dorothea. "Hm. Yes . . ." Comment on "Leading Generously," Humanities Commons, August 2022.

Schein, Edgar H., and Peter A. Schein. *Humble Inquiry: The Gentle Art of Asking Instead of Telling.* 2nd ed. Berrett-Koehler, 2021.

Schulze, Robin. "Interview." November 2021.

Senge, Peter M. *The Fifth Discipline: The Art and Practice of the Learning Organization.* Doubleday, 2006.

Settles, Isis H., Martinque K. Jones, NiCole T. Buchanan, and Kristie Dotson. "Epistemic Exclusion: Scholar(ly) Devaluation That Marginalizes Faculty of Color." *Journal of Diversity in Higher Education* 14, no. 4 (December 2021): 493–507.

Shaw, Madeleine. *The Greater Good: Social Entrepreneurship for Everyday People Who Want to Change the World.* Wonderwell, 2021.

Skinner, Katherine. "Embracing Change." Educopia Institute, July 2022.

———. "Interview." March 2021.

Snyder, Barbara. "AAU President Expresses Deep Concern about Michigan State University Trustees' Interference in School Operations." Association of American Universities, September 2022. https://www.aau.edu /newsroom/press-releases/aau-president-expresses-deep-concern-about -michigan-state-university.

Snyder, Timothy. *On Tyranny: Twenty Lessons from the Twentieth Century.* Tim Duggan Books, 2017.

Solnit, Rebecca. *Hope in the Dark: Untold Histories, Wild Possibilities.* Updated ed. Haymarket Books, 2016.

Spade, Dean. *Mutual Aid: Building Solidarity During This Crisis (and the Next).* Verso Books, 2020.

Stack, Jack, with Bo Burlingham. *The Great Game of Business: The Only Sensible Way to Run a Company.* Random House, 2013.

State News Editorial Board, The. "EDITORIAL: We're Not Going to Class Monday." *The State News* [MSU], February 2023.

Stripling, Jack, and Susan Svrluga. "Colleges Want Open Doors. MSU Shooting Shows the Risk." *Washington Post,* February 2023.

Táíwò, Olúfẹ́mi O. *Elite Capture: How the Powerful Took Over Identity Politics (and Everything Else).* Haymarket Books, 2022.

Taplin, Jonathan. *Move Fast and Break Things: How Facebook, Google, and Amazon Cornered Culture and Undermined Democracy.* Illustrated ed. Little, Brown, 2017.

Tsing, Anna Lowenhaupt. *The Mushroom at the End of the World: On the Possibility of Life in Capitalist Ruins.* Princeton University Press, 2015.

United States Department of Education. "Predominantly Black Institutions Program—Formula Grants." September 2016. https://www2.ed.gov/programs/pbihea/index.html.

Utell, Janine. "Thinking about Two Things Here . . ." Comment on "Leading Generously," Humanities Commons, September 2022.

Valamis. "Shared Leadership." Sec. "What Is Shared Leadership?" Valamis, updated March 2023. https://www.valamis.com/hub/shared-leadership.

Vise, Daniel de, and Anita Kumar. "U-Va. Board Leaders Wanted President Teresa Sullivan to Make Cuts." *Washington Post*, June 17, 2012.

Warzel, Charlie, and Anne Helen Petersen. *Out of Office: The Big Problem and Bigger Promise of Working from Home*. Knopf, 2021.

Weinzweig, Ari. *A Lapsed Anarchist's Approach to Being a Better Leader*. Zingerman's Press, 2012.

White, Timothy P. "Message from the Office of the Chancellor." September 2020

Young, Iris Marion. *Justice and the Politics of Difference*. Princeton University Press, 2011.

Zimmerman, Jess. "Why Is Male Anger So Threatening?" *Dame Magazine*, March 2017.

Index

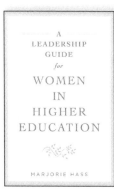